THE MOLDAU FAMILY EDITION

THE FOUR CUPS
הגדה של פסח

A Recovery Haggadah

NUSACH ASHKENAZ

Edited by **RABBI SHAIS TAUB**
Author of **God of Our Understanding**

THE FOUR CUPS
A RECOVERY HAGGADAH

Published and Copyrighted © 2021

by
Shais & Schuster
978-977-9111 | Info@fourcups.org
www.fourcups.org

Orders:
978-977-9111 | Info@fourcups.org
www.fourcups.org

Your submissions for future editions: submissions@fourcups.org

The main Haggadah text and translation is presented here, with permission, from Rabbi Chaim Miller's *Kol Menachem Haggadah, Nusach Ashkenaz*.

All rights reserved. No part of this publication may be reproduced, stored in a retrieval system, or transmitted in any form or by any means, electronic, mechanical, photocopying, recording, or otherwise, without prior permission from the copyright holder.

Sources: Rabbi Aaron L. Raskin
Design and Layout: Spotlight Design, Brooklyn, NY
Illustrations: Leba Muchnik

ISBN: 978-168524681-5

Printed in China

IN EVERY GENERATION AND EVERY DAY WE OUGHT
TO SEE OURSELVES AS IF WE LEFT EGYPT.
(MISHNAH PESACHIM 10:5)

Passover celebrates our People's liberation and redemption from Egypt and ever since has served as a guiding light for anyone who seeks liberation and redemption in their personal life.

As we approach Passover we pray for all those who are on a journey of recovery, liberation, and redemption.

It is our hope that this Haggadah serves as a valuable tool for all those on this journey.

DAVID AND HARRIET MOLDAU

DEDICATED TO OUR DEAR FAMILY, CHILDREN, AND GRANDCHILDREN PRESENT AND FUTURE

ALEXANDRE & PAULA WEINSTEIN

IN LOVING MEMORY OF OUR SON
JEFF (MOISHE) KRAUS

INTRODUCTION

OUR MIRACULOUS REDEMPTION from slavery is a fundamental concept in the identity, belief, and daily practice of the Jewish people.[1] There is not a day that goes by on which we are not obligated to remember what God did for us in taking us out of Egypt.[2] Additionally, we make special mention of the Exodus on every Shabbos and festival.

But why is liberation from slavery such a central theme in Judaism?

Over the ages, many explanations have been given. However, to those of us in the recovery community, the answer is quite obvious: We understand our relationship with God as a personal story of slavery and freedom. It was our bondage to self that forced us to look in earnest for a Power greater than ourselves. And it is because of the miraculous daily redemption that He performs for us that we are most acutely aware of His continuing presence in our lives. Without having gone through our own slavery and redemption experience, we wonder if we would be as aware of our relationship with God as we are today. We are almost sure that we wouldn't be.

It is in this spirit of profound appreciation for our collective and personal exodus that we bring to you *The Four Cups: A Recovery Haggadah*.

INTRODUCTION

This Haggadah follows the traditional format with the classic text as has been accepted over the millennia. As grateful recipients of our sacred heritage, we have approached the traditional text with reverence and have taken great care to preserve it in its traditional and cherished format.

At the same time, we have been moved to offer our own personal experience as it relates to the themes of Passover. You will find our own "experience, strength, and hope" shared in the commentary that appears underneath the standard traditional text.

These reflections and insights are the collective offering of many men and women in recovery. We cannot attribute authorship to any one individual; rather, these are ideas that have been shared by many of us at various times. Accordingly, we have also chosen to write this commentary in the first-person plural ("we").

Where appropriate, we have included endnotes to classic sources—both scriptural and rabbinic—which will aid the reader in further study.

The submissions were reviewed and edited by Rabbi Shais Taub, who tried to preserve a uniform voice throughout the commentary while also allowing the uniqueness of each entry to speak for itself.

The title of this Haggadah was chosen in order to convey a subtle but powerful message. The role of the four cups in the Seder is well known. For those who cannot safely consume wine because of its alcoholic content, the question arises as to how one should view this tradition. Of course, on a very simple and practical level, we know that it is perfectly acceptable according to Jewish law to substitute grape juice for wine at the Seder. On a deeper level, however, we acknowledge that one who does not drink wine might wonder if it would be better to be completely distanced from the entire notion of drinking four cups, even if replaced with grape juice.

Therefore, we feel that there is an important message in making it clear that the four cups not only have a place at a recovery Seder, but that they perhaps take on an even greater meaning in such a context. The four cups are meant to be cups of blessing from which Godly goodness flows. Although we may have replaced the physical

INTRODUCTION

contents of the cup with grape juice instead of wine, we do not forgo the spiritual contents of the cups and the blessings that they provide us. To the contrary—we are even more cognizant of their power.

For someone still struggling to escape the Egypt of active addiction, the image of four cups is one that provokes dread. However, for one who celebrates the miracle of today's freedom from bondage, the four cups have a very different meaning. They are cups of spiritual bounty of wisdom, humility, and gratitude.

We drink from these cups freely, because their contents do not make false promises of escape. Rather, they fill us with ever-increasing levels of God-consciousness and the awareness that the only reason we are no longer slaves to Pharaoh is that we are servants of God.

To submit your suggestions for review for a future edition, please email your insights to submissions@fourcups.org.

הגדה של פסח

Editor's Foreword

It is not without some degree of hesitation that I lend my name to this book. One of the foundational principles of recovery is principles above personalities. However, after much deliberation, it was decided that I should come forward and let my connection with this work be known.

So let me clarify what I can and cannot take credit for: The insights that make up the commentary in this Haggadah are the collective contribution of countless Jews in recovery who are sharing their personal experience, strength, and hope. As such, it is impossible to attribute authorship of this book to any one person.

As a rabbi with a passion for the message of recovery, I was enlisted to review the contributions to ensure their accuracy and then combine them into a single coherent work with a somewhat consistent voice.

Much more critical than my role as editor was that of Rabbi Nechemia Schusterman, who coordinated the entire project from beginning to end. Rabbi Schusterman tirelessly fit all of the pieces of the puzzle together, from content to design to bringing the final work to publication. May Hashem reward his work with infinite blessings for him and his entire family.

EDITOR'S FOREWORD

It should be noted that *The Four Cups: A Recovery Haggadah* is very much a work in progress, and it is the intention of the editors to produce further editions, with Hashem's help, so that we can include the perspectives of more coauthors. Surely, "more will be revealed."

Regarding the use of Nusach Ashkenaz for the text, this Haggadah was designed to be a fully functional Haggadah that one can actually use at the Seder. Although the differences between the various traditional rites are fairly minor, they are certainly noticeable to those familiar with the text. We apologize to those who may be inconvenienced by this choice. Ultimately our editorial decision was made based on what we hope will promote the greatest ease of use by the greatest number of people.

At the time of the printing of this book, we are still within the first year of the passing of a singular figure within the Jewish recovery world, our beloved Rabbi Dr. Abraham J. Twerski, of blessed memory. It is safe to say that without Rabbi Dr. Twerski's work, this Haggadah would not exist. He was the one who brought to light not only the problem of addiction in the Jewish world, but the solution of recovery as well. With wisdom and compassion, he gave us the gift of his teachings and showed us a path to freedom.

This Haggadah is dedicated to his everlasting memory.

Rabbi Shais Taub
Cedarhurst, NY

THE SEARCH FOR CHAMETZ

- On the eve of 14 Nissan (the night before the Seder), inspect the house for Chametz. (If the eve of the 14th occurs on Shabbos, the search is carried out on Thursday night, and the burning on Friday morning.)

- Many have a custom to place tiny (wrapped) pieces of bread in various places around the house (according to Kabbalah, ten pieces).

- Search with the light of a wax candle. It is customary to collect the Chametz with a feather and wooden spoon.

- Before the search, recite the following blessing and start to search without speaking. After this blessing, until the search is completed, you may speak only about matters relevant to the search.

- A superficial search will not suffice. Be careful to check all the corners, nooks, and crannies of the rooms that require searching, as well as pockets in all clothing.

Revealing Our Defects of Character

On the night before Passover, we are obligated to search for the Chametz in our homes.

Traditionally, the search for Chametz is performed with a feather, a wooden spoon, and a candle.

The following day, on the morning before the festival commences, we make a fire and burn the Chametz we have found, along with the feather, the spoon, and the candle.

It is easy to understand why we burn the feather that was used to sweep the Chametz that was found, as well as why we burn the spoon into which the Chametz was swept. But why do we burn the candle? After all, it did not come in contact with the Chametz at all.

One explanation is that the candle was needed to help us find the Chametz, but after it serves its purpose, we must get rid

THE SEARCH FOR CHAMETZ

בָּרוּךְ אַתָּה יְהֹוָה אֱלֹהֵינוּ מֶלֶךְ הָעוֹלָם, אֲשֶׁר קִדְּשָׁנוּ בְּמִצְוֹתָיו וְצִוָּנוּ עַל בִּעוּר חָמֵץ:

Blessed are You, God, our God, King of the universe, Who has sanctified us with His commandments and commanded us about the disposal of Chametz.

- After the search, wrap the Chametz carefully and safeguard until tomorrow. Any Chametz foods that are to be eaten tomorrow should be kept in a safe place.

- Now recite the following declaration, relinquishing any remaining Chametz that was not found (or sold) from your possession. If you do not understand Aramaic, you must say it in English.

כָּל חֲמִירָא וַחֲמִיעָא דְּאִכָּא בִרְשׁוּתִי, דְּלָא חֲמִיתֵּהּ וּדְלָא בְעַרְתֵּהּ וּדְלָא יְדַעֲנָא לֵיהּ, לִבְטֵל וְלֶהֱוֵי הֶפְקֵר כְּעַפְרָא דְאַרְעָא.

All leaven and leavened products that are in my possession that I did not observe, did not dispose of, or do not know about, are hereby nullified and ownerless, like the dust of the earth.

---

of it, as well, because it was involved in shedding light upon that which is undesirable.[3]

There's a man who sponsors many alcoholics. Following the tradition that was handed down to him by his sponsor, he has his sponsees burn their written Fourth Step inventories after he takes their Fifth Step.

He explained that the purpose of the inventory is to reveal the "exact nature of our wrongs."

After it serves its purpose, we don't need to go back and look at it. We need to move forward and allow God to replace our character defects with the traits that He finds useful.

THE DISPOSAL OF CHAMETZ

- On the following morning (see a local Jewish calendar for the specific timing, which varies from year to year), burn all the remaining (unsold) Chametz.

- After the Chametz has been burned in the fire, recite the following declaration, relinquishing any remaining Chametz from your possession. If you do not understand Aramaic, you must say it in English.

כָּל חֲמִירָא וַחֲמִיעָא דְּאִכָּא בִרְשׁוּתִי דַּחֲזִתֵּהּ וּדְלָא חֲזִתֵּהּ דַּחֲמִתֵּהּ וּדְלָא חֲמִתֵּהּ דְּבִעַרְתֵּהּ וּדְלָא בִעַרְתֵּהּ לִבְטֵל וְלֶהֱוֵי הֶפְקֵר כְּעַפְרָא דְאַרְעָא.

All leaven and leavened products that are in my possession, which I did or did not see, which I did or did not observe, or which I did or did not dispose of, are hereby nullified and ownerless, like the dust of the earth.

THE ORDER OF THE HAGGADAH

- Matzah: Take three whole Shmurah Matzos and place them one on top of the other, separated by napkins. (Many have the custom to insert the Matzos into compartments under the Seder plate.)
- The Seder plate is then arranged according to your family custom. (The predominant custom is to follow the arrangement of the Arizal, displayed below.)
- Some have the custom to bring the Seder plate to the table before Kiddush, while others bring it after Kiddush.

1. SHANKBONE: The shoulder bone of a lamb with some meat on it, roasted.

2. EGG: A roasted or boiled egg.

3. BITTER HERBS: Grated horseradish.

4. CHAROSES: A thick paste of ground apples, nuts, other fruits, wine or grape juice, and cinnamon.

5. KARPAS: Celery, parsley, radishes, or boiled potato.

6. CHAZERES: Romaine lettuce.

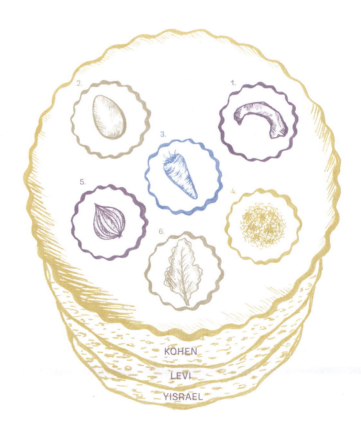

KOHEN
LEVI
YISRAEL

THE PESACH SEDER
STEPS

קדש		KADESH
ורחץ		URCHATZ
כרפס		KARPAS
יחץ		YACHATZ
מגיד		MAGGID
רחצה		RACHTZAH
מוציא		MOTZI
מצה		MATZAH
מרור		MAROR
כורך		KORECH
שולחן עורך		SHULCHAN ORECH
צפון		TZAFUN
ברך		BARECH
הלל		HALLEL
נרצה		NIRTZAH

Good Orderly Direction

We begin the Seder by enumerating the precise steps that we will be taking in our journey to freedom. We realize that in the past many of us have resisted being confined by lists or being given orders to follow.

However, in sobriety, many of us have come to cherish the freedom that we gain through taking direction. Indeed, the word "Seder" itself literally means "order" in Hebrew. Is it ironic that a night that celebrates freedom is observed by following an order? We think not.

Many of us have heard in the rooms that GOD can be thought of as an acronym for Good Orderly Direction. Therefore, we are very happy to know that the system has been laid out for us and that the fifteen steps of our liberation are set up clearly in advance.

 **SEDER STEP 1 KADESH**

KADESH

- It is customary for the head of the household to wear a white Kittel during the Seder.
- Kiddush may not be started until nightfall.
- As a display of freedom, each person should have their cup filled by someone else.
- On Friday and Saturday night, instead say the Kiddush text provided on pages 19 to 20.

סַבְרִי מָרָנָן וְרַבָּנָן וְרַבּוֹתַי:
בָּרוּךְ אַתָּה יְהֹוָה אֱלֹהֵינוּ מֶלֶךְ הָעוֹלָם, בּוֹרֵא פְּרִי הַגָּפֶן:

Attention, my masters and teachers!

Blessed are You, God, our God, King of the universe, Who creates the fruit of the vine.

בָּרוּךְ אַתָּה יְהֹוָה אֱלֹהֵינוּ מֶלֶךְ הָעוֹלָם, אֲשֶׁר בָּחַר בָּנוּ מִכָּל־עָם וְרוֹמְמָנוּ מִכָּל־לָשׁוֹן וְקִדְּשָׁנוּ בְּמִצְוֹתָיו, וַתִּתֶּן־לָנוּ יְהֹוָה אֱלֹהֵינוּ בְּאַהֲבָה מוֹעֲדִים לְשִׂמְחָה, חַגִּים

Blessed are You, God, our God, King of the universe, Who has chosen us from among all nations, and raised us above all tongues, and sanctified us through His commandments. And You, God, our God, have lovingly given us festivals for rejoicing, holidays, and

Kadesh is the first step of our journey. This step is the recitation of the Kiddush blessings. "Kiddush" literally means "sanctification." With these blessings, we proclaim this day — the anniversary of our liberation—as a holy day.

In Jewish tradition, a holy day is observed as a day of Shabbos-like rest, during which we refrain from mundane activities and labors. Of course, this allows us more time to

Humbly Letting Go

וּזְמַנִּים לְשָׂשׂוֹן, אֶת־יוֹם חַג הַמַּצּוֹת הַזֶּה, זְמַן חֵרוּתֵנוּ, מִקְרָא קֹדֶשׁ, זֵכֶר לִיצִיאַת מִצְרָיִם. כִּי בָנוּ בָחַרְתָּ וְאוֹתָנוּ קִדַּשְׁתָּ מִכָּל־הָעַמִּים, וּמוֹעֲדֵי קָדְשֶׁךָ בְּשִׂמְחָה וּבְשָׂשׂוֹן הִנְחַלְתָּנוּ: בָּרוּךְ אַתָּה יְהֹוָה, מְקַדֵּשׁ יִשְׂרָאֵל וְהַזְּמַנִּים:

seasons to be cheerful—the day of this Festival of Matzos, the time of our freedom, pronounced holy, as a memorial of the Exodus from Egypt. For You have chosen us and sanctified us above all the nations. And Your holy festivals, in rejoicing and cheerfulness, You have given us as an inheritance. Blessed are You, God, Who sanctifies Israel and the seasons.

Do not repeat this blessing if you said it at candle lighting.

בָּרוּךְ אַתָּה יְהֹוָה אֱלֹהֵינוּ מֶלֶךְ הָעוֹלָם, שֶׁהֶחֱיָנוּ וְקִיְּמָנוּ וְהִגִּיעָנוּ לַזְּמַן הַזֶּה:

Blessed are You, God, our God, King of the universe, Who has kept us alive, sustained us, and brought us to this season.

- Recline to the left and drink the entire cup (or at least the majority of it), preferably without pausing.

focus on spiritual affairs, but there's another message to be found here, as well.

When we refrain from labor on a special day, we remind ourselves that our ability to accomplish things is limited. Many of us have heard the expression, "Don't just do something; sit there!" Sometimes, we have to humbly accept the limitations of our actions and realize that there's a difference between being busy and being productive.

A festival is a day when the less busy we are, the more productive we actually become. 🍷

KADESH

KIDDUSH FOR FRIDAY/SATURDAY NIGHT

Instead of the Kiddush on pages 17 to 18, say the following;
On Friday night add the purple text:

(say quietly: And it was evening and it was morning)

The Sixth Day. The skies, the earth, and all their numerous components were completed. On the seventh day, God completed His work that He had made. On the seventh day, He rested from all His work that He had done. God blessed the seventh day and He sanctified it, because on it God rested from all His work that He had created, to make.

Attention, my masters and teachers!

Blessed are You, God, our God, King of the universe, Who creates the fruit of the vine.

Blessed are You, God, our God, King of the universe, Who has chosen us from among all nations, and raised us above all tongues, and sanctified us through His commandments. And You, God, our God, have lovingly given us (Shabbos for rest) festivals for rejoicing, holidays, and seasons to be cheerful—(this Shabbos day and) the day of this Festival of Matzos, the time of our freedom, pronounced holy (in love), as a memorial of the Exodus from Egypt. For You have chosen us and sanctified us above all the nations. And Your holy (Shabbos and) Festivals, which (lovingly and willingly), with rejoicing and

(say quietly: וַיְהִי־עֶרֶב וַיְהִי־בֹקֶר)

יוֹם הַשִּׁשִּׁי: וַיְכֻלּוּ הַשָּׁמַיִם וְהָאָרֶץ וְכָל־צְבָאָם: וַיְכַל אֱלֹהִים בַּיּוֹם הַשְּׁבִיעִי מְלַאכְתּוֹ אֲשֶׁר עָשָׂה, וַיִּשְׁבֹּת בַּיּוֹם הַשְּׁבִיעִי מִכָּל־מְלַאכְתּוֹ אֲשֶׁר עָשָׂה: וַיְבָרֶךְ אֱלֹהִים אֶת־יוֹם הַשְּׁבִיעִי וַיְקַדֵּשׁ אֹתוֹ, כִּי בוֹ שָׁבַת מִכָּל־מְלַאכְתּוֹ אֲשֶׁר־בָּרָא אֱלֹהִים לַעֲשׂוֹת:

סַבְרִי מָרָנָן וְרַבָּנָן וְרַבּוֹתַי:

בָּרוּךְ אַתָּה יְהֹוָה אֱלֹהֵינוּ מֶלֶךְ הָעוֹלָם, בּוֹרֵא פְּרִי הַגָּפֶן:

בָּרוּךְ אַתָּה יְהֹוָה אֱלֹהֵינוּ מֶלֶךְ הָעוֹלָם, אֲשֶׁר בָּחַר בָּנוּ מִכָּל־עָם וְרוֹמְמָנוּ מִכָּל־לָשׁוֹן וְקִדְּשָׁנוּ בְּמִצְוֹתָיו, וַתִּתֶּן־לָנוּ יְהֹוָה אֱלֹהֵינוּ בְּאַהֲבָה (שַׁבָּתוֹת לִמְנוּחָה וּ) מוֹעֲדִים לְשִׂמְחָה, חַגִּים וּזְמַנִּים לְשָׂשׂוֹן, (אֶת־יוֹם הַשַּׁבָּת הַזֶּה וְ) אֶת־יוֹם חַג הַמַּצּוֹת הַזֶּה, זְמַן חֵרוּתֵנוּ, (בְּאַהֲבָה) מִקְרָא קֹדֶשׁ, זֵכֶר לִיצִיאַת מִצְרָיִם. כִּי בָנוּ בָחַרְתָּ וְאוֹתָנוּ קִדַּשְׁתָּ מִכָּל־הָעַמִּים, (וְשַׁבָּת) וּמוֹעֲדֵי קָדְשֶׁךָ (בְּאַהֲבָה וּבְרָצוֹן) בְּשִׂמְחָה

וּבְשָׂשׂוֹן הִנְחַלְתָּנוּ: בָּרוּךְ אַתָּה יְהֹוָה, מְקַדֵּשׁ (הַשַּׁבָּת וְ) יִשְׂרָאֵל וְהַזְּמַנִּים:

cheerfulness, You have given us as an inheritance. Blessed are You, God, Who sanctifies (the Shabbos and) Israel and the seasons.

On Saturday night add the following text:

בָּרוּךְ אַתָּה יְהֹוָה אֱלֹהֵינוּ מֶלֶךְ הָעוֹלָם, בּוֹרֵא מְאוֹרֵי הָאֵשׁ:
בָּרוּךְ אַתָּה יְהֹוָה אֱלֹהֵינוּ מֶלֶךְ הָעוֹלָם, הַמַּבְדִּיל בֵּין קֹדֶשׁ לְחוֹל, בֵּין אוֹר לְחֹשֶׁךְ, בֵּין יִשְׂרָאֵל לָעַמִּים, בֵּין יוֹם הַשְּׁבִיעִי לְשֵׁשֶׁת יְמֵי הַמַּעֲשֶׂה. בֵּין קְדֻשַּׁת שַׁבָּת לִקְדֻשַּׁת יוֹם טוֹב הִבְדַּלְתָּ, וְאֶת־יוֹם הַשְּׁבִיעִי מִשֵּׁשֶׁת יְמֵי הַמַּעֲשֶׂה קִדַּשְׁתָּ, הִבְדַּלְתָּ וְקִדַּשְׁתָּ אֶת־עַמְּךָ יִשְׂרָאֵל בִּקְדֻשָּׁתֶךָ: בָּרוּךְ אַתָּה יְהֹוָה, הַמַּבְדִּיל בֵּין קֹדֶשׁ לְקֹדֶשׁ:

Blessed are You, God, our God, King of the universe, Who creates the lights of fire.
Blessed are You, God, our God, King of the universe, Who distinguishes between sacred and mundane, between light and darkness, between Israel and the nations, between the seventh day and the six workdays. You have distinguished between the holiness of the Shabbos and the holiness of the Festival, and You have sanctified the seventh day above the six workdays. You have distinguished and sanctified Your people Israel with Your holiness. Blessed are You, God, Who distinguishes between holy and holy:

Do not repeat this blessing if you said it at candle lighting.

בָּרוּךְ אַתָּה יְהֹוָה אֱלֹהֵינוּ מֶלֶךְ הָעוֹלָם, שֶׁהֶחֱיָנוּ וְקִיְּמָנוּ וְהִגִּיעָנוּ לַזְּמַן הַזֶּה:

Blessed are You, God, our God, King of the universe, Who has kept us alive, sustained us, and brought us to this season.

- Recline to the left and drink the entire cup (or at least the majority of it), preferably without pausing.

SEDER STEP 2
URCHATZ

WASH THE HANDS

- The head of the household washes their hands without making a blessing (see below). (In many households, the Seder participants also wash their hands).
- It is customary for the head of the household to have the water brought to their seat.

How to wash:

- Before washing the hands check that they are clean and dry.
- Pour plenty of water (at least three ounces) twice over your right hand so that the water covers the entire hand up to the wrist.
- Pass the container into your right hand and pour water twice over your left hand, exactly as before.
- Let go of the container and dry your hands thoroughly.
- Do not make a blessing.

We Know Only a Little

Generally on Shabbos and festivals, Kiddush is followed with washing our hands and then beginning our meal. Tonight, however, we wash our hands, but we do not begin our meal.

This is specifically intended to provoke the curiosity of the children, so that they will ask why this night is different from all others.[4]

One of the lessons we learned in sobriety is, "We realize we know only a little."[5]

It is okay for us not to understand things. It is okay for us to be confused, and it is okay for us to ask questions.

This is not only for the literal child present at our Seder, but also for the child in each of us.

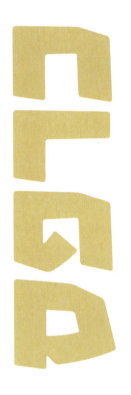

SEDER STEP 3
KARPAS

DIP & EAT THE VEGETABLE

- Do not take a vegetable that may be used for bitter herbs.
- Dip a small piece of vegetable (less than 0.9 oz.) into salt water, make the following blessing, and then eat it. Have in mind that this blessing also applies to all the bitter herbs eaten later. (Most people do not lean.)

בָּרוּךְ אַתָּה יְהֹוָה אֱלֹהֵינוּ מֶלֶךְ הָעוֹלָם, בּוֹרֵא פְּרִי הָאֲדָמָה:

Blessed are You, God, our God, King of the universe, Who creates the fruit of the earth.

Feel the Pain

At this point we dip a piece of vegetable into salt water, which symbolizes the tears we shed as slaves in Egypt.[6]

We know that while in active addiction many of us were afraid to feel, and we used our drug of choice to numb our emotions so we would not have to experience pain.

Tonight, as we experience our liberation, we do not avoid the tears.

We allow ourselves to feel the pain of slavery as well as the exhilaration of redemption.

SEDER STEP 4
YACHATZ

BREAK THE MIDDLE MATZAH

- Break the middle Matzah into two, one piece bigger than the other.
- Remove the larger piece (now designated as the Afikoman), wrap it in a cloth, and set it aside.
- The smaller piece of Matzah is left between the two whole Matzos.
- Some place the Afikoman briefly on their shoulders (to remember how the Jewish people left Egypt with Matzos on their shoulders).

Embracing Our Brokenness

Before we begin to tell the story of our liberation, we first break the middle Matzah. One of the reasons for this is that the Haggadah must be recited over "poor man's bread."[7]

It is not enough that the Matzah is already flat—symbolizing humility. It must also be broken.

To us, this is an obvious truth: that humility and brokenness are prerequisites to a journey toward freedom.

 **SEDER STEP 5**
MAGGID

TELL THE EXODUS STORY

- The Seder plate is lifted up with the Matzos uncovered.
- The Haggadah should be recited loudly, joyously, and with intense concentration. It is customary that every person reads along out loud.

Telling Our Story

Maggid—which has the same Hebrew root as Haggadah—means "telling the story." In our own recovery we have experienced the healing power of telling our personal stories and of hearing others tell theirs.

We realize that in telling our story, things that seemed unbearable at the time—things that we thought we could not live through—take on a completely new meaning in retrospect. There is no event, no experience, that cannot be redeemed and elevated when framed as a story.

Notably, it is in telling our story that we also make ourselves useful to others. We know that the very first Twelve-Step program, Alcoholics Anonymous, began when one drunk told his personal story to another. Bill W. did not try to talk to Dr. Bob about the latter's drinking. Instead, he spoke about his own experience with drinking and the solution that he had found. Therefore, when the two of them went to AA number 3, they did not sermonize or exhort him. They simply told him their own personal stories.

We heal ourselves and others when we tell our story.

MAGGID

This is the bread of affliction

הָא לַחְמָא עַנְיָא

דִּי אֲכָלוּ אַבְהָתָנָא בְּאַרְעָא דְמִצְרָיִם. כָּל־דִּכְפִין יֵיתֵי וְיֵיכוֹל, כָּל־דִּצְרִיךְ יֵיתֵי וְיִפְסַח. הָשַׁתָּא הָכָא, לְשָׁנָה הַבָּאָה בְּאַרְעָא דְיִשְׂרָאֵל. הָשַׁתָּא עַבְדֵי, לְשָׁנָה הַבָּאָה בְּנֵי חוֹרִין:

that our ancestors ate in the land of Egypt. All who are hungry, let them come and eat! All who are needy, let them come and conduct the Passover Seder! Now we are here; next year we will be in the Land of Israel. Now we are slaves; next year we will be free people.

Open to All

Before we officially begin our Seder, we proclaim that it is open to all. "All who are hungry, let them come and eat. All who are needy, let them come and conduct the Passover Seder!" In other words, the only requirement for membership at the Seder is a desire to be here.

Furthermore, we remember that the most important person at the meeting is the newcomer. When we celebrate our freedom, it is not by sequestering ourselves in some elite or exclusive group; rather, it is by being as inclusive as possible. So we open our homes and hearts to whomever may wish to partake of our celebration of freedom.

Notice that we say, "Now we are slaves, next year we will be free people." Isn't the point of the Seder to celebrate that we are already free?

One explanation is that we say this as a poignant reminder of our interconnectedness—that as long as there are those who still suffer inside or outside of these walls, our own freedom is also limited.

Until all of us are free, none of us are completely liberated. And so we open our Seder to all. 🍷

- The Matzos are covered and the tray is removed (or pushed to the side). The cup of wine is filled for the second time.
- The following is asked by the youngest child.

מַה־נִּשְׁתַּנָּה הַלַּיְלָה הַזֶּה מִכָּל־הַלֵּילוֹת.

Why is this night different from all other nights?

שֶׁבְּכָל־הַלֵּילוֹת אָנוּ אוֹכְלִין חָמֵץ וּמַצָּה, הַלַּיְלָה הַזֶּה כֻּלּוֹ מַצָּה:

On all other nights we eat Chametz or Matzah, but on this night only Matzah!

The True Father

In many Haggadahs there is a line of instruction before the four questions. It states in Hebrew, Kan Haben Sho'eil, which literally means "here the son asks."

The Hebrew word for "ask" can also be translated as "borrow." Accordingly, this can be read as "here the son borrows." What does this mean?

One explanation is that if a child does not have a father to whom to ask the four questions, they can "borrow God" as their father. God Almighty Himself makes Himself available to each one of us.

We may have been disappointed by human beings, and we have various excuses of how they let us down, but we have come to find that our problem was never going to be solved by human power anyway.

Regardless of what we think we are lacking in our human relationships, we must know that we can find what we're looking for in our relationship with God.

MAGGID

שֶׁבְּכָל־הַלֵּילוֹת אָנוּ אוֹכְלִין שְׁאָר יְרָקוֹת, הַלַּיְלָה הַזֶּה מָרוֹר:

On all other nights we eat any kind of vegetables, but on this night bitter herbs!

שֶׁבְּכָל־הַלֵּילוֹת אֵין אָנוּ מַטְבִּילִין אֲפִילוּ פַּעַם אֶחָת, הַלַּיְלָה הַזֶּה שְׁתֵּי פְעָמִים:

On all other nights we do not dip even once, but on this night we do so twice!

שֶׁבְּכָל־הַלֵּילוֹת אָנוּ אוֹכְלִין בֵּין יוֹשְׁבִין וּבֵין מְסֻבִּין, הַלַּיְלָה הַזֶּה כֻּלָּנוּ מְסֻבִּין:

On all other nights we eat sitting upright or reclining, but on this night we all recline!

Don't Rationalize the Darkness

On a deeper, mystical level, the question "Why is this night different?" refers to the darkness of our people's exile.[8]

We were exiled in Egypt for two hundred and ten years. We were exiled in Babylonia for seventy years. The current exile since the destruction of the Second Temple has been going on for nearly two thousand years.

So we ask our Father in heaven, "Why is this night—this exile—different from all others? Why is it so long? Why is it so brutal? Why are the troubles we face so unprecedented?"

This question is not necessarily meant to elicit an answer. Rather, the question itself has value.

When we are in a situation of doubled and redoubled darkness, the greatest danger is to begin to think that darkness is really light. Our capacity for rationalization catches up with the chaos around us and tells us that what was once unacceptable is somehow manageable and normal.

We must never forget that it was the admission of unmanageability that started us on our path to freedom. When we are in a place of darkness, we must not be complacent. We must call out to God and at the very least ask the question "Why is this night different?"

מַצָּה

- The Seder plate is returned to its place and the three Matzos are partially uncovered.

We were slaves to Pharaoh in Egypt,

עֲבָדִים הָיִינוּ לְפַרְעֹה בְּמִצְרַיִם,

וַיּוֹצִיאֵנוּ יְהֹוָה אֱלֹהֵינוּ מִשָּׁם בְּיָד חֲזָקָה וּבִזְרֹעַ נְטוּיָה.

but God, our God, took us out from there with a strong hand and with an outstretched arm.

וְאִלּוּ לֹא הוֹצִיא הַקָּדוֹשׁ בָּרוּךְ הוּא אֶת־אֲבוֹתֵינוּ מִמִּצְרַיִם, הֲרֵי אָנוּ וּבָנֵינוּ וּבְנֵי בָנֵינוּ מְשֻׁעְבָּדִים הָיִינוּ לְפַרְעֹה בְּמִצְרָיִם.

If the Holy One, blessed be He, had not taken our ancestors out of Egypt, then we, our children, and our children's children would still be enslaved to Pharaoh in Egypt.

Beyond Human Aid

Our story begins: "We were slaves to Pharaoh in Egypt." That much we know already. But it is the following line that may surprise us: "If the Holy One, blessed be He, had not taken our ancestors out of Egypt, then we, our children, and our children's children would still be enslaved to Pharaoh in Egypt."

This is a startling revelation.

Not only were we unable to extricate ourselves from Egypt, but what we are being told here is that we would *never* have been able to do so, even if given centuries and millennia; it was simply impossible.[9] No human power could have ever removed us from Egypt.

Therefore, if God Himself had not removed us, we would still be slaves there to this day.

MAGGID

וַאֲפִילוּ כֻּלָּנוּ חֲכָמִים כֻּלָּנוּ נְבוֹנִים כֻּלָּנוּ זְקֵנִים כֻּלָּנוּ יוֹדְעִים אֶת־הַתּוֹרָה, מִצְוָה עָלֵינוּ לְסַפֵּר בִּיצִיאַת מִצְרָיִם. וְכָל־הַמַּרְבֶּה לְסַפֵּר בִּיצִיאַת מִצְרַיִם הֲרֵי זֶה מְשֻׁבָּח:

Even if we were all people of wisdom, people of understanding, experienced and knowledgeable in the Torah, we would still be obligated to tell the story of the Exodus from Egypt. And whoever discusses the Exodus from Egypt at length is praiseworthy.

Keeping It Green

"Even if we were all people of wisdom, people of understanding, experienced and knowledgeable in the Torah, we would still be obligated to tell the story of the Exodus from Egypt."

We mentioned earlier that "Haggadah" means "telling,"[10] and one of the main Mitzvos tonight is to tell our story. These lines of the Haggadah reinforce the idea that telling our story is not something that is only necessary in early sobriety.

Even if we were all wise and understanding and knew the entire Torah—no matter what level of spiritual growth we attain—we still need to know where we came from and be able to relate that narrative to others. Some refer to this as "keeping it green," meaning that even as we reach new spiritual frontiers, we keep the memories of early recovery fresh in our minds. ♦

It's Happening Now

Another interpretation of the term "to tell the story of the Exodus from Egypt" is based on a rereading of the original Hebrew words to mean "to go out of Egypt through relating our story."

This is not simply a memory. It is not even a reenactment. We realize the power of retelling our story actually causes us to experience deeper levels of freedom each time we tell it.

Therefore, Kol Hamarbeh—anyone who increases in telling this story is praiseworthy. ♦

מַגִּיד

מַעֲשֶׂה בְּרַבִּי אֱלִיעֶזֶר וְרַבִּי יְהוֹשֻׁעַ וְרַבִּי אֶלְעָזָר בֶּן־עֲזַרְיָה וְרַבִּי עֲקִיבָא וְרַבִּי טַרְפוֹן שֶׁהָיוּ מְסֻבִּין בִּבְנֵי בְרַק,

It once happened that Rabbi Eliezer, Rabbi Yehoshua, Rabbi Elazar ben Azaryah, Rabbi Akiva, and Rabbi Tarfon were reclining at a Seder in Bnei Brak.

Working with Others

At first glance, there are a number of odd things about this story.

First of all, why are the students interrupting their teachers in the middle of their telling of the story? It hardly seems like proper conduct.

Second, why are they interrupting to tell them something that is obvious to anyone who looks out the window? The time of the morning Shema is when the sun begins to shine. No one needs to be told that.

However, this story is teaching us a very important lesson about the need to work with newcomers.

You see, we have just learned that regardless of our level of spiritual growth—even if we were all wise, understanding, and knew the entire Torah—we would still have to keep telling our story.

And that is precisely what the Sages were doing. They were up all night telling each other the Exodus story in an attempt to inspire one another.

The challenge they were facing was that precisely because they were on such a high spiritual level, there was very little

MAGGID

They were discussing the Exodus from Egypt that entire night, until their students came and said to them: "Teachers! The time has come for reciting the morning Shema!"

וְהָיוּ מְסַפְּרִים בִּיצִיאַת מִצְרַיִם כָּל־אוֹתוֹ הַלַּיְלָה עַד שֶׁבָּאוּ תַלְמִידֵיהֶם וְאָמְרוּ לָהֶם: "רַבּוֹתֵינוּ, הִגִּיעַ זְמַן קְרִיאַת שְׁמַע שֶׁל שַׁחֲרִית":

they had not already heard or understood. Nothing was novel or exciting to them. So they stayed up all night talking to each other, trying to get inspired, but they weren't able to do so.

That is when the students interrupted and said, "Teachers! The time has come for reciting the morning Shema!": You have illuminated matters for us. The sun is shining, and it's time to proclaim the Oneness of God![11]

The students were telling the Sages, in essence, "Although everything you are telling each other may be old to you, it is new to us. You might not be inspired, but you've inspired us. The sun is now shining for us! The Oneness of God is now clear to us!"

The lesson for us is that sometimes we reach a place in our spiritual growth where our spiritual routine becomes familiar, and we are unable to feel the original excitement of early sobriety. We have to know that when we work with a newcomer and manage to inspire them, it is just as if we have been inspired anew, as well.

מַגִּיד

Rabbi Elazar ben Azaryah said:

אָמַר רַבִּי אֶלְעָזָר בֶּן־עֲזַרְיָה:

הֲרֵי אֲנִי כְּבֶן־שִׁבְעִים שָׁנָה, וְלֹא זָכִיתִי שֶׁתֵּאָמֵר יְצִיאַת מִצְרַיִם בַּלֵּילוֹת עַד שֶׁדְּרָשָׁהּ בֶּן זוֹמָא, שֶׁנֶּאֱמַר: "לְמַעַן תִּזְכֹּר אֶת־יוֹם צֵאתְךָ מֵאֶרֶץ מִצְרַיִם כֹּל יְמֵי חַיֶּיךָ."

"יְמֵי חַיֶּיךָ" — הַיָּמִים.

"כֹּל יְמֵי חַיֶּיךָ" — הַלֵּילוֹת.

I am like a seventy-year-old man and I did not yet merit [to find a Scriptural proof that in addition to the daytime obligation] to mention the Exodus from Egypt [there is also an obligation to mention it] every night—until [today, when] Ben Zoma demonstrated a proof from the following verse: "That you should remember the day you left Egypt all the days of your life."[12]

[Ben Zoma explained that if the verse would merely have stated,] "the days of your life," there would already be a sufficient proof for a daytime obligation [to mention the Exodus]. The fact that the verse stresses "all the days of your life" indicates a further obligation [to mention the Exodus] in the evenings.

Quality of Sobriety

Historically we know that Rabbi Elazar ben Azaryah was only eighteen years old when this story occurred.[13]

What does it mean that he was like a man of seventy?

There are many explanations for this passage. One lesson that is obvious to us is that there are those who are relative newcomers but whose quality of sobriety is well beyond their years.

Many of us have even heard the saying that "the one in the room with the most sobriety is the one who got up earliest this morning."

Although we celebrate milestones and birthdays, we don't judge sobriety merely by a number. There can be someone with a relatively recent sobriety date who is advanced in their spiritual growth, and we should humble ourselves to receive from such people when they share with us. 🍷

MAGGID

The Sages said:

"The days of your life," would be sufficient to include the current era.

[The fact that the verse states] "all the days of your life," includes [also an obligation to mention the Exodus in the Messianic Era.

וַחֲכָמִים אוֹמְרִים:

"יְמֵי חַיֶּיךָ" — הָעוֹלָם הַזֶּה.

"כֹּל יְמֵי חַיֶּיךָ" — לְהָבִיא לִימוֹת הַמָּשִׁיחַ:

What It Was Like

What were the Sages clarifying by explaining that we will continue to recall the Exodus even after the advent of the Messianic Era?

The simple explanation is that one might think that after the future redemption occurs, the redemption from Egypt will pale so much in comparison that it will no longer be worthy of mention.

We are therefore told that no matter what spiritual heights we collectively attain, we will always remember our liberation from our first exile—the Exodus from Egypt.

Spiritual growth is a continuum. It is not something that happens once; rather, it is ongoing—increasing over time.

We remind ourselves that regardless of how good life gets, we will always remember the early days of sobriety—our first redemption, when we originally went from slavery to freedom.

Additionally, the Exodus from Egypt was not only chronologically the first redemption, but it is the paradigm for all future redemptions and made them all possible.[14]

As we grow and experience more of the gifts that sobriety has to offer, we do not forget the beginning of our journey.

We realize that our initial admission of powerlessness is still very much relevant to our lives. We have not outgrown it. On the contrary, we bring it with us and recall it constantly. By keeping the memories of the past fresh, we ensure the quality of our sobriety today.

מַגִּיד

בָּרוּךְ הַמָּקוֹם בָּרוּךְ הוּא,

Blessed is the All-present One!

בָּרוּךְ שֶׁנָּתַן תּוֹרָה לְעַמּוֹ יִשְׂרָאֵל, בָּרוּךְ הוּא.

כְּנֶגֶד אַרְבָּעָה בָנִים דִּבְּרָה תוֹרָה: אֶחָד חָכָם, וְאֶחָד רָשָׁע, וְאֶחָד תָּם, וְאֶחָד שֶׁאֵינוֹ יוֹדֵעַ לִשְׁאוֹל:

Blessed is He! Blessed is He Who gave the Torah to His people Israel. Blessed is He!

The Torah speaks of four children: one wise, one wicked, one simple, and one who does not know how to ask.

Those Who Are Not Here

We speak of four types of children at the Seder—the wise child, the wicked child, the simple child, and the child who does not know how to ask. We reflect on the fact that even the wicked child, with the hostile questions, is still, after all, present at the Seder. The wicked child may be here under protest, but at least the wicked child is still here—arguing, complaining, fighting, but still here.

We must remember that there is an unspoken fifth child, who is not even in attendance at the Seder. We must ask ourselves what we are doing to reach these lost children.

There are many who need to be in the room but aren't yet. It is our job to carry the message—as the Twelfth Step instructs—and bring in the "fifth child."

At this time, we will have a moment of silence for those still suffering outside of these walls.

חָכָם מַה הוּא אוֹמֵר?
The wise child: what does this child say?

"מָה הָעֵדֹת וְהַחֻקִּים וְהַמִּשְׁפָּטִים אֲשֶׁר צִוָּה יְהֹוָה אֱלֹהֵינוּ אֶתְכֶם?"

"What are these commemorative laws, suprarational laws, and civil laws that God, our God, has commanded you?"[15]

וְאַף אַתָּה אֱמָר־לוֹ כְּהִלְכוֹת הַפֶּסַח: "אֵין מַפְטִירִין אַחַר הַפֶּסַח אֲפִיקוֹמָן":

You should instruct them in the laws of the Paschal lamb: "We do not serve any dessert after the Paschal lamb."[16]

Carrying the Message

The order of the four children is exact, and many things can be learned just from their placement.

Where is the wise child seated? Right next to the so-called "wicked child."

There is an important reason for this. The presence of the wise child at the Seder is not merely for that child's own benefit; rather, it is also to share their experience, strength, and hope with those who may need it.

The wise child is therefore placed next to the wicked child, in the hope that the wise child will be able to be of service to them.[17]

It is sometimes overlooked that one of the best places to carry the message and perform our Twelfth Step is *at* a meeting.

We do not attend meetings just because of the help that we need to receive; it is also, and perhaps more importantly, because of the help we are able to give. The wise child's placement next to the wicked child reminds us of that.

A Simple Program (for Complicated People)

Alternatively, there is another lesson to be gleaned from the placement of the wise child next to the wicked one.

The wise child should remember that they are not so very far off from the wicked child. "There, but for the grace of God, go I," the wise child should think.

Indeed, being a wise child is often fraught with peril.

רָשָׁע מַה הוּא אוֹמֵר?
The wicked child: what does this child say?

"מָה הָעֲבוֹדָה הַזֹּאת לָכֶם?" "What is this ritual service to you?"[18]

Overthinking is a common trap that can put one's spiritual fitness at risk. The wise child specifically has to remember the importance of keeping it simple.

This is also the significance of the answer that we give the wise child—that we don't eat anything after the Afikoman.

In Hebrew, the word for "taste" is "Ta'am," which also means "reason."[19]

The wise child, with their great intellect, enjoys understanding the reasons behind everything. They therefore need to be told that at the end of the Seder they will be left with the bland taste of Matzah in their mouth, and they will not have the opportunity to seek more exciting fare.

Metaphorically, we are telling the wise child that sometimes we need to stick to simplicity, accept the limitations of our knowledge, and be comfortable with the fact that we do not have all the answers.

A Message to the Terminally Unique

Why do we refer to any of the four children disparagingly—as "wicked"? It is important to understand that the so-called "wicked child" is only wicked by their own estimation.

From the wording of their question and the description of it that the Haggadah gives—"What is this ritual service to you? 'To you,' but not to themself"—this child removes themself from the community. It is clear that their real problem is seeing themself as completely disconnected from what is going on. In other words, their wickedness is not a label that we use to condemn them, God forbid. Rather, the Haggadah is telling

"**לָכֶם**" וְלֹא לוֹ. וּלְפִי שֶׁהוֹצִיא אֶת־עַצְמוֹ מִן הַכְּלָל, כָּפַר בְּעִקָּר.

וְאַף אַתָּה הַקְהֵה אֶת־שִׁנָּיו וֶאֱמָר־לוֹ: "בַּעֲבוּר זֶה עָשָׂה יְהוָה לִי בְּצֵאתִי מִמִּצְרָיִם." "**לִי**" וְלֹא לוֹ, אִלּוּ הָיָה שָׁם לֹא הָיָה נִגְאָל:

"To you," but not to themself. In declaring immunity from the law, they've denied a basic principle of Judaism.

You should therefore also blunt their teeth and say: "It is because of this that God did for me when I left Egypt."[20] "For me," but not for them! If they had been there, they would not have been redeemed.

us something quite different. It is telling us that feeling terminally unique ("But my case is different—no one understands") is the one sin that makes it impossible to recover.

We may then ask why the response to this person is seemingly so harsh—we "blunt their teeth."

To understand this, we must realize that the Haggadah was originally written in Hebrew and that it is a particular style of Hebrew filled with hidden codes.

Every Hebrew letter has a numerical value. The numerical value of the word for "wicked," "Rasha," is five hundred and seventy. If we subtract the value of the Hebrew word for "Shinav"—"his teeth"—which is three hundred and sixty-six, we get the Hebrew word for "righteous," "Tzaddik."[21]

So the encoded hidden message is that we don't throw the wicked one out even though they feel that there is nothing for them to gain at this gathering. We respond to them in a way that may seem harsh. But really, all we are trying to do is to reveal their inner righteous person. We do not coddle them, but we remove from them this feeling of being "terminally unique," thereby revealing the righteousness hidden within them all along.

| ר | ש | ע | 570 |
| 70 | 300 | 200 | |

| ש | נ | י | ו | 366 |
| 6 | 10 | 50 | 300 | |

| צ | ד | י | ק | 204 |
| 100 | 10 | 4 | 90 | |

תָּם מַה הוּא אוֹמֵר?
The simple child: What does this child say?

"מַה־זֹּאת?" וְאָמַרְתָּ אֵלָיו: "בְּחֹזֶק יָד הוֹצִיאָנוּ יְהוָֹה מִמִּצְרַיִם מִבֵּית עֲבָדִים":

"What is this?" Say back: "With a strong hand God took us out of Egypt, from the house of slavery."[22]

Keep It Simple

In many ways, the simple child is the unsung hero of the Haggadah. Much commentary has been written about the wise child and the wicked child. Perhaps the simple child has been overlooked.

In our spiritual journey, we have come to cherish the value of simplicity.

The simple child's question is two words in Hebrew: "Mah Zos?—What's this?" This child cannot articulate a more sophisticated way of asking. And yet, the answer the parent gives is incredibly inspiring. It is simple but clear:

"B'chozek Yad Hotzianu Hashem MiMitzrayim Mibeis Avadim—With a strong hand God took us out of Egypt, from the house of slavery."

The simple question of the simple child elicits a simple truth—that God did for us what we could not do for ourselves.

MAGGID

וְשֶׁאֵינוֹ יוֹדֵעַ לִשְׁאוֹל:
With the child who does not know how to ask:

You must take the initiative, as the verse states: "You shall tell your child on that day, saying, 'It is because of this that God did for me when I left Egypt.'"[23]

אַתְּ פְּתַח לוֹ, שֶׁנֶּאֱמַר: "וְהִגַּדְתָּ לְבִנְךָ בַּיּוֹם הַהוּא לֵאמֹר, בַּעֲבוּר זֶה עָשָׂה יְהוָה לִי בְּצֵאתִי מִמִּצְרָיִם":

The Prospect Who Doesn't Know How to Ask

When it comes to the child who doesn't know how to ask, we are told the parent is supposed to initiate by telling them the story of our redemption.

We know that there are those who still suffer, who aren't even able to reach out for help.

When we suspect that we are talking to such a prospect, we do not wait for them to initiate. Rather, we tell them the story of our miraculous redemption, and we hope that it will resonate with them—if not now, then perhaps with the passage of time.

One might יָכוֹל

מֵרֹאשׁ חֹדֶשׁ – תַּלְמוּד לוֹמַר: "בַּיּוֹם הַהוּא." אִי בַּיּוֹם הַהוּא, יָכוֹל מִבְּעוֹד יוֹם – תַּלְמוּד לוֹמַר "בַּעֲבוּר זֶה": "בַּעֲבוּר זֶה" לֹא אָמַרְתִּי אֶלָּא בְּשָׁעָה שֶׁיֵּשׁ מַצָּה וּמָרוֹר מֻנָּחִים לְפָנֶיךָ:

think [that the discussion of the Exodus story] must be from the beginning of the month. The Torah therefore says, "[You shall tell your child] on that day."[24] However, "On that day" could mean while it is still daytime [when the Paschal lamb is offered]. The Torah therefore states [the additional words], "Because of this"—i.e., only when Matzah and bitter herbs are placed before you.

Sobriety Date

In this paragraph, the Haggadah describes a matter of debate among the Sages regarding the proper date on which to celebrate the anniversary of our redemption from Egypt.

An argument can be made that we should observe this occasion on the day when we were told that we would leave Egypt, which was the first day of the month of Nissan. Another argument can be made that it should be observed on the day before we left. However, the Haggadah concludes that we do not mark the anniversary until the day when we actually left.

We, in sobriety, know the significance of a "sobriety date"—the anniversary of our leaving Egypt. Of course, when we look back, we can see how there were many events that led to our first day of sobriety. But the actual date of leaving Egypt is not until "our first twenty-four hours."

MAGGID

מִתְּחִלָּה עוֹבְדֵי עֲבוֹדָה זָרָה הָיוּ אֲבוֹתֵינוּ, וְעַכְשָׁו קֵרְבָנוּ הַמָּקוֹם לַעֲבֹדָתוֹ. שֶׁנֶּאֱמַר: "וַיֹּאמֶר יְהוֹשֻׁעַ אֶל־כָּל־הָעָם, כֹּה־אָמַר יְהוָֹה אֱלֹהֵי יִשְׂרָאֵל: בְּעֵבֶר הַנָּהָר יָשְׁבוּ אֲבוֹתֵיכֶם מֵעוֹלָם, תֶּרַח אֲבִי אַבְרָהָם וַאֲבִי נָחוֹר, וַיַּעַבְדוּ אֱלֹהִים אֲחֵרִים":

In the beginning, our ancestors were idol-worshippers, but now the All-present One has brought us close to God's worship, as the verse states: "Joshua said to all the people, this is what God, the God of Israel, said: 'Your ancestors used to live across the river—Terach, Abraham's father and Nachor's father—and they served foreign gods.

We Will Not Regret The Past

"Our ancestors were idol-worshippers." Why do we mention this unseemly detail about our past?

The Talmud[25] tells us that the story of the redemption—in fulfilling the mitzvah to retell it—must begin with disgrace.

But why is it important to start our stories there? Why can't we just begin with the glorious miracles of redemption?

For those of us who have experienced our personal exodus, it is obvious why our story must begin with disgrace.

We do not revel in the sordid details of the past. At the same time, however, we feel that to not include this part of our story would be to seemingly minimize the greatness of the miracles God has done for us.

Therefore, we read, "In the beginning our ancestors were idol-worshippers, but *now* the All-present One has brought us close to God's worship."

That sentence can be read not only as two separate events—one coming first and the other coming second—but as a cause and effect. Because we fell so low, God has now brought us so close.

"וָאֶקַּח אֶת־אֲבִיכֶם אֶת־אַבְרָהָם מֵעֵבֶר הַנָּהָר, וָאוֹלֵךְ אוֹתוֹ בְּכָל־אֶרֶץ כְּנָעַן, וָאַרְבֶּה אֶת־זַרְעוֹ וָאֶתֶּן־לוֹ אֶת־יִצְחָק: וָאֶתֵּן לְיִצְחָק אֶת־יַעֲקֹב וְאֶת־עֵשָׂו, וָאֶתֵּן לְעֵשָׂו אֶת־הַר שֵׂעִיר לָרֶשֶׁת אוֹתוֹ, וְיַעֲקֹב וּבָנָיו יָרְדוּ מִצְרָיִם:"

"'But I took your patriarch Abraham from across the river, and I led him through the whole land of Cana'an. I multiplied his offspring, and I gave him Isaac; and to Isaac I gave Jacob and Esau. To Esau I gave Mount Sei'ir to possess it, and Jacob and his sons went down to Egypt'"[26]

Healing That Reaches Back Through Time

Does the story of the Exodus need to include events that happened centuries prior? Why are we told about the lives of Abraham, Isaac, and Jacob, who lived generations before the Exodus?

Perhaps the lesson is that for those of us who are fortunate enough to experience personal redemption, we should remember that it is not only us but all of the generations who came before us who are experiencing redemption along with us.

Many of us believe strongly that our spiritual awakening has brought healing to intergenerational trauma that we may not even know about. Our story isn't confined to our own lifetimes. It is a story that reaches back through the ages and brings healing to those who lived before us.

MAGGID

בָּרוּךְ שׁוֹמֵר הַבְטָחָתוֹ / Blessed is He

לְיִשְׂרָאֵל בָּרוּךְ הוּא, שֶׁהַקָּדוֹשׁ בָּרוּךְ הוּא חִשַּׁב אֶת־הַקֵּץ לַעֲשׂוֹת כְּמָה שֶׁאָמַר לְאַבְרָהָם אָבִינוּ בִּבְרִית בֵּין הַבְּתָרִים. שֶׁנֶּאֱמַר:

Who keeps His promise to the Jewish people! Blessed is He! For the Holy One, blessed be He, calculated the end when He would carry out what He had told our patriarch Abraham at the Covenant of the Parts, as the verse states:

Grateful Addict

Why was the servitude in Egypt revealed to Abraham generations before it happened?

And why is he then told that, after everything they will go through, his descendants will leave their servitude with great wealth?

Wouldn't it be better for them to never have to go through it at all? And if they do have to go through it, what is the point in telling Abraham such discouraging news?

However, we must reframe the way we view our years of bondage in Egypt.

Yes, it was a terrible descent. But it was a descent for the sake of a subsequent ascent.

No one wants to be told that their child is going to be an addict. However, many of us appreciate that the levels that one can reach through recovery could not have been reached any other way.

In that regard, Abraham is being told very good news. That his descendants will experience the lowest levels of spiritual bankruptcy in Egypt, but this will directly bring them to new heights that could not have been reached any other way.

מגיד

"וַיֹּאמֶר לְאַבְרָם, יָדֹעַ תֵּדַע כִּי גֵר יִהְיֶה זַרְעֲךָ בְּאֶרֶץ לֹא לָהֶם וַעֲבָדוּם וְעִנּוּ אֹתָם, אַרְבַּע מֵאוֹת שָׁנָה: וְגַם אֶת־הַגּוֹי אֲשֶׁר יַעֲבֹדוּ דָּן אָנֹכִי, וְאַחֲרֵי־כֵן יֵצְאוּ בִּרְכֻשׁ גָּדוֹל":

"And He said to Abram, 'You should know that your descendants will be strangers in a land that is not theirs, where they will be enslaved and oppressed for four hundred years. Then I will pronounce judgment on the nation whom they will serve, and afterwards they will leave with great wealth.'"[27]

- Cover the Matzos and hold the cup in your hand.

MAGGID

And it is this
וְהִיא שֶׁעָמְדָה

לַאֲבוֹתֵינוּ וְלָנוּ, שֶׁלֹּא אֶחָד בִּלְבָד עָמַד עָלֵינוּ לְכַלּוֹתֵנוּ, אֶלָּא שֶׁבְּכָל־דּוֹר וָדוֹר עוֹמְדִים עָלֵינוּ לְכַלּוֹתֵנוּ, וְהַקָּדוֹשׁ בָּרוּךְ הוּא מַצִּילֵנוּ מִיָּדָם:

that has stood by our ancestors and us! For not just one alone has risen against us to destroy us, but in each and every generation they rise against us to destroy us—and the Holy One, blessed be He, saves us from their hand!

- Place the cup back on the table and uncover the Matzos.

Our Miraculous Existence

We recall at this point that the near annihilation of our people in Egypt was not the last time that we were in peril. In every generation, our people faced yet another seemingly insurmountable challenge that by all rights should have been the end of us. We remember this, because to do so is to acknowledge that our very existence is the result of miracle after miracle.

No ancient people has been through what we have been through and is still here to tell the tale. The only reason why we sit here today and recall everything that we and our ancestors have been through is that God has repeatedly shown us miracles in every generation.

We sit here today as the beneficiaries of a chain of miracles.

Let us take a moment now to reflect that not only has God performed miracles personally for us in our lives but throughout the ages, as well, and it is because of these miracles that we are even here today.

מַגִּיד

צֵא וּלְמַד מַה־בִּקֵּשׁ לָבָן הָאֲרַמִּי לַעֲשׂוֹת לְיַעֲקֹב אָבִינוּ, שֶׁפַּרְעֹה לֹא גָזַר אֶלָּא עַל הַזְּכָרִים וְלָבָן בִּקֵּשׁ לַעֲקוֹר אֶת־הַכֹּל, שֶׁנֶּאֱמַר:

Go out and learn what Laban the Aramean wanted to do to our patriarch Jacob. Pharaoh only decreed against the males, but Laban wanted to eliminate everyone, as the verse states:

The Big Lie

What makes Laban a greater villain than Pharaoh?

One of the things the Torah tells us about Laban is that he told Jacob, who was his son-in-law, "Your children are my children. Your sons are my sons. Your daughters are my daughters."[33]

What he meant to say was that although he had abused Jacob and taken advantage of him, he wanted Jacob to give him credit as if he were the one responsible for all his success. In other words, Laban's message was, "I've given you everything. You can never make it on your own. You're nothing without me."

Many of us relate to the idea that the insidious lure of addiction was what it was able to do for us. It made us feel like we could accomplish things we could never have accomplished before on our own.

But then it began to demand a central place in our lives. No longer was it serving us; it wanted us to serve it. It wanted us to admit that we have no life without it and that everything good was only because it had allowed us to have it.

In demanding that we acknowledge its total power over us, the disease of addiction seeks to, like Laban, "uproot everything." It tells us that we can never have peace without it. And it demands that we give ourselves over to it with our very lives.

Our response must be like Jacob's response to Laban, namely that Jacob realizes that Laban's claims are all bluff and that Laban has no real power over him. Despite our addiction telling us that we cannot live without it, the very opposite is true. Life begins when we break free from its spell.

MAGGID

"אֲרַמִּי אֹבֵד אָבִי, וַיֵּרֶד מִצְרַיְמָה וַיָּגָר שָׁם בִּמְתֵי מְעָט, וַיְהִי־שָׁם לְגוֹי גָּדוֹל עָצוּם וָרָב":

"An Aramean sought to destroy my father. He went down to Egypt and sojourned there, few in number; and he became a nation there—great, mighty, and numerous."[28]

"וַיֵּרֶד מִצְרַיְמָה" – אָנוּס עַל־פִּי הַדִּבּוּר.

"He went down to Egypt" — compelled by Divine decree.

"וַיָּגָר שָׁם" – מְלַמֵּד שֶׁלֹּא יָרַד יַעֲקֹב אָבִינוּ לְהִשְׁתַּקֵּעַ בְּמִצְרַיִם אֶלָּא לָגוּר שָׁם,

"And [he] sojourned there" — This teaches that our patriarch Jacob did not go down to settle in Egypt,

A Subtle Foe

The beginning of our two hundred and ten years in Egypt seemed harmless enough. Jacob went down there to be reunited with his family; he had no intention of staying, let alone that generations of his descendants would end up living there, as well. As it says, "He did not go down with the intention of settling but rather to visit."

When we look back at our story and our descent into our own bondage, it is clear to us that we never intended to become captives. We thought we were merely visiting and that we could come and go as we pleased.

We are reminded that, for most of us, the descent into absolute servitude was gradual and seemed quite harmless at the time.

More importantly, we remember how easy it is to slip back into slavery now if we are not careful. Therefore, we are ever vigilant about enlarging our spiritual lives so that we don't wake up one day and realize we have enslaved ourselves again.

שֶׁנֶּאֱמַר: "וַיֹּאמְרוּ אֶל פַּרְעֹה לָגוּר בָּאָרֶץ בָּאנוּ, כִּי־אֵין מִרְעֶה לַצֹּאן אֲשֶׁר לַעֲבָדֶיךָ כִּי־כָבֵד הָרָעָב בְּאֶרֶץ כְּנָעַן, וְעַתָּה יֵשְׁבוּ־נָא עֲבָדֶיךָ בְּאֶרֶץ גֹּשֶׁן":

"בִּמְתֵי מְעָט" — כְּמָה שֶׁנֶּאֱמַר: "בְּשִׁבְעִים נֶפֶשׁ יָרְדוּ אֲבֹתֶיךָ מִצְרָיְמָה, וְעַתָּה שָׂמְךָ יְהֹוָה אֱלֹהֶיךָ כְּכוֹכְבֵי הַשָּׁמַיִם לָרֹב":

but only to live there temporarily, as the verse states: "They said to Pharaoh, 'We have come to sojourn in the land, for your servants' flocks have no pasture, since the famine is severe in the Land of Cana'an. Now please, let your servants settle in the Land of Goshen.'"[29]

"Few in number" — As the verse states: "When your forebears went down to Egypt they were seventy souls, but now God, your God, has made you as numerous as the stars of the skies."[30]

Our Miraculous Growth

We recall that when our forefather Jacob and his family first arrived in Egypt, they were few in number: only seventy souls, to be precise.[34] And yet despite being targeted for persecution, they multiplied greatly into an entire nation of people within a relatively short amount of time.

It is easy to forget sometimes how relatively recent the entire recovery movement phenomenon is. It was not so many decades ago that a New York stockbroker met an Akron physician in his home and shared with him a message that they would then go on to share with others. The rapidness with which their simple program of action spread is something of a modern miracle.

It is helpful to consider the fact that, although those who are actually in recovery are a much smaller number than those who may need recovery, we should not become despondent. With God, our numbers can increase rapidly and exponentially even under the most harrowing of conditions.

MAGGID

"And he became a nation there"— This teaches that the Israelites were recognizably distinct there.

"Great, mighty" — As the verse states: "And the Children of Israel were fruitful and swarmed and increased and became very, very strong; and the land became filled with them."[31]

"And numerous"— As the verse states: "I caused you to thrive like the plants of the field, and you increased, and grew, and became very adorned, your bosom fashioned and your hair grown long; yet you were naked and bare. When I passed over you and saw you weltering in your bloods, I said to you, 'By your blood you shall live,' and I said to you, 'By your blood shall you live!'"[32]

"וַיְהִי־שָׁם לְגוֹי" – מְלַמֵּד שֶׁהָיוּ יִשְׂרָאֵל מְצֻיָּנִים שָׁם:

"גָּדוֹל עָצוּם" – כְּמָה שֶׁנֶּאֱמַר: "וּבְנֵי יִשְׂרָאֵל פָּרוּ וַיִּשְׁרְצוּ וַיִּרְבּוּ וַיַּעַצְמוּ בִּמְאֹד מְאֹד, וַתִּמָּלֵא הָאָרֶץ אֹתָם":

"וָרָב" – כְּמָה שֶׁנֶּאֱמַר: "רְבָבָה כְּצֶמַח הַשָּׂדֶה נְתַתִּיךְ, וַתִּרְבִּי וַתִּגְדְּלִי וַתָּבוֹאִי בַּעֲדִי עֲדָיִים, שָׁדַיִם נָכֹנוּ וּשְׂעָרֵךְ צִמֵּחַ, וְאַתְּ עֵרֹם וְעֶרְיָה: וָאֶעֱבֹר עָלַיִךְ וָאֶרְאֵךְ מִתְבּוֹסֶסֶת בְּדָמָיִךְ, וָאֹמַר לָךְ בְּדָמַיִךְ חֲיִי וָאֹמַר לָךְ בְּדָמַיִךְ חֲיִי":

מגיד

"וַיָּרֵעוּ אֹתָנוּ הַמִּצְרִים וַיְעַנּוּנוּ, וַיִּתְּנוּ עָלֵינוּ עֲבֹדָה קָשָׁה":

"The Egyptians treated us badly, they made us suffer, and they imposed hard labor upon us!"[35]

"וַיָּרֵעוּ אֹתָנוּ הַמִּצְרִים" — כְּמָה שֶׁנֶּאֱמַר: "הָבָה נִתְחַכְּמָה לוֹ, פֶּן־יִרְבֶּה וְהָיָה כִּי־תִקְרֶאנָה מִלְחָמָה וְנוֹסַף גַּם־הוּא עַל־שֹׂנְאֵינוּ וְנִלְחַם־בָּנוּ וְעָלָה מִן־הָאָרֶץ":

"וַיְעַנּוּנוּ" — כְּמָה שֶׁנֶּאֱמַר: "וַיָּשִׂימוּ עָלָיו שָׂרֵי מִסִּים

"The Egyptians treated us badly"— As the verse states: "Come, let us act cunningly with them lest they increase. For if a war will occur, they will join our enemies, fight against us, and depart from the land."[36]

"They made us suffer" — As the verse states: "They appointed taskmasters over them to afflict

An Invisible Line

It is true that the Egyptians placed back-breaking labor upon us, but our tradition reveals that there is more to the story. Our Sages[39] tell us that originally Pharaoh made a call for volunteers to join in a public project of city building. In other words, the Jewish people were not forced to show up at first. They responded voluntarily. However, when they wanted to leave, the taskmaster suddenly appeared and told them that they could not.

This pattern is not unfamiliar to us. Many of us can recall a time when our drug of choice was something we could "take or leave" as we pleased. We felt that we were doing so voluntarily and of our own free will. However, there came a day when we wanted to stop and realized that the choice was no longer our own. At that point, only a Power greater than ourselves could restore our power of choice.

"לְמַעַן עַנֹּתוֹ בְּסִבְלֹתָם, וַיִּבֶן עָרֵי מִסְכְּנוֹת לְפַרְעֹה אֶת־פִּתֹם וְאֶת־רַעַמְסֵס": them with their burdens, and they built storage cities for Pharaoh: Pisom and Ra'amses."37

"וַיִּתְּנוּ עָלֵינוּ עֲבֹדָה קָשָׁה" — כְּמָה שֶׁנֶּאֱמַר: "וַיַּעֲבִדוּ מִצְרַיִם אֶת־בְּנֵי יִשְׂרָאֵל בְּפָרֶךְ": "And they imposed hard labor upon us" — As the verse states: "The Egyptians enslaved the Children of Israel with crushing labor."38

An Easier, Softer Way

The Haggadah tells us that the Egyptians enslaved the Jews "with crushing labor." What was uniquely crushing about the labor the Jews were forced to engage in? Our tradition tells us that the cities the Jewish people were forced to build were built upon swampland. Every day they would toil their utmost, and the next morning they would return to the worksite only to find that everything that they had built the previous day had sunk into the ground. Therefore, what was so crushing was not the degree of hard work but its inherent pointlessness. No matter how hard they worked, their work was ultimately unproductive.

Is a life of sobriety any less work than a life of active addiction?

Many of us have said that however hard you worked on feeding your addiction is how hard you have to work on maintaining your sobriety. So sobriety does not excuse us from hard work. The difference is that we are now working toward goals that actually pay off. In the past we frittered away untold time and energy chasing the elusive dream that something artificial and outside of ourselves could make us feel okay. That was like building on swampland. The results never remained for long.

Now, in contrast, we invest our efforts into being of service to our Maker and to others. We find that every bit of work we expend toward that goal is well worth the trouble. Therefore, the difference between slavery and freedom is not the degree of hard work but the productivity of the work itself. We work hard in recovery, but the work is infinitely rewarding.

מגיד

"וַנִּצְעַק אֶל־יְהֹוָה אֱלֹהֵי אֲבֹתֵינוּ, וַיִּשְׁמַע יְהֹוָה אֶת־קֹלֵנוּ וַיַּרְא אֶת־עָנְיֵנוּ וְאֶת־עֲמָלֵנוּ וְאֶת־לַחֲצֵנוּ:"

"And we cried out to God, the God of our ancestors. God heard our voice and He saw our affliction, our toil, and our oppression."[40]

"וַנִּצְעַק אֶל־יְהֹוָה אֱלֹהֵי אֲבֹתֵינוּ" — כְּמָה שֶׁנֶּאֱמַר: "וַיְהִי בַיָּמִים הָרַבִּים הָהֵם וַיָּמָת מֶלֶךְ מִצְרַיִם, וַיֵּאָנְחוּ בְנֵי־יִשְׂרָאֵל מִן־הָעֲבֹדָה וַיִּזְעָקוּ, וַתַּעַל שַׁוְעָתָם אֶל־הָאֱלֹהִים מִן־הָעֲבֹדָה:"

"And we cried out to God, the God of our ancestors" — As the verse states: "After many days had passed, the king of Egypt died. The Children of Israel groaned from the hard work, and they cried out. And their prayers, prompted by the hard work, rose up to God."[41]

There's One Who Has All Power

At this point in the narrative, as we are telling the story of our slavery and redemption, things take a sudden and dramatic turn. Whereas for generations we were toiling under the brutal Pharaoh, seemingly with no end in sight, we are suddenly told that God heard our cries.

Rabbi Dr. Twerski of blessed memory once related how a newcomer asked an old-timer to share with him his secret of sobriety. "It's simple," said the old-timer. "At the end of every day, I thank God for having given me another day of sobriety today, and I ask Him for another day of sobriety tomorrow." The newcomer then wondered aloud: "And how do you know that it was God Who gave you that day of sobriety?"

The old-timer looked at him in puzzlement. "It had to be. I didn't ask anyone else."

MAGGID

"God heard our voice" — As the verse states: "God heard their cry, and God remembered His covenant with Abraham, Isaac, and Jacob."[42]

"And He saw our affliction" — ["our affliction"] referring to the separation of husband and wife — as the verse states: "God saw the Children of Israel, and God took note."[43]

"Our toil" — This means [the decree against] the children, as the verse states: "Every boy who is born you shall cast into the Nile, and every girl you shall keep alive."[44]

"And our oppression" — This means the pressure, as the verse states: "And I have also seen the oppression with which the Egyptians are oppressing them."[45]

"וַיִּשְׁמַע יְהֹוָה אֶת־קֹלֵנוּ" — כְּמָה שֶׁנֶּאֱמַר: "וַיִּשְׁמַע אֱלֹהִים אֶת־נַאֲקָתָם, וַיִּזְכֹּר אֱלֹהִים אֶת־בְּרִיתוֹ אֶת־אַבְרָהָם אֶת־יִצְחָק וְאֶת־יַעֲקֹב":

"וַיַּרְא אֶת־עָנְיֵנוּ" — זוֹ פְּרִישׁוּת דֶּרֶךְ אֶרֶץ — כְּמָה שֶׁנֶּאֱמַר: "וַיַּרְא אֱלֹהִים אֶת־בְּנֵי יִשְׂרָאֵל וַיֵּדַע אֱלֹהִים":

"וְאֶת־עֲמָלֵנוּ" — אֵלּוּ הַבָּנִים — כְּמָה שֶׁנֶּאֱמַר: "כָּל־הַבֵּן הַיִּלּוֹד הַיְאֹרָה תַּשְׁלִיכֻהוּ וְכָל־הַבַּת תְּחַיּוּן":

"וְאֶת־לַחֲצֵנוּ" — זוֹ הַדְּחָק — כְּמָה שֶׁנֶּאֱמַר: "וְגַם־רָאִיתִי אֶת־הַלַּחַץ אֲשֶׁר מִצְרַיִם לֹחֲצִים אֹתָם":

May You Find Him Now

After two hundred and ten years of slavery, what made the difference so that God finally intervened?

The Haggadah tells us clearly, "And we cried out."

There were many human attempts to leave Egypt. Slaves tried to escape on their own and failed. What was different this time was that we finally realized that we could never leave Egypt by our own power.

We cried out to God, and God heard our cries. It is at this point that everything changed.

מגיד

"וַיּוֹצִאֵנוּ יְהֹוָה מִמִּצְרַיִם בְּיָד חֲזָקָה וּבִזְרֹעַ נְטוּיָה וּבְמֹרָא גָּדֹל וּבְאֹתוֹת וּבְמֹפְתִים":

"God brought us out of Egypt with a strong hand, with an outstretched arm, with great awe, with signs, and with wonders."[46]

"וַיּוֹצִאֵנוּ יְהֹוָה מִמִּצְרַיִם" — לֹא עַל יְדֵי מַלְאָךְ, וְלֹא עַל יְדֵי שָׂרָף, וְלֹא עַל יְדֵי שָׁלִיחַ, אֶלָּא הַקָּדוֹשׁ בָּרוּךְ הוּא בִּכְבוֹדוֹ וּבְעַצְמוֹ, שֶׁנֶּאֱמַר:

"God brought us out of Egypt"— Not through an angel, not through a seraph, and not through a messenger; rather, it was the Holy One, blessed be He, He himself in His glory, as the verse states: "I will pass

A Different Basis

When God redeemed us from Egypt, not only did He topple the evil regime of Pharaoh; He disgraced all of the false gods of Egypt as well. Why was it important to show the ineffectiveness of the Egyptian idols?

After two hundred and ten years in Egypt, our people had become assimilated. They were not only impressed with the Egyptians and their way of life but with their "higher powers," as well. It was therefore not enough that we witness the greatness of God. We needed to see the uselessness of the idols as well.

Our stories as individuals certainly testify to the greatness of God in our lives. We should also remember that our stories show the utter impotence of powers other than God. Not only do we, as sober people, rely on God; we reject all powers that give false hope. That doesn't just mean the empty promises of our drug of choice; rather, as we progress in sobriety, we realize that this means any power in this world other than the Highest Power.

"through the land of Egypt on this night, and I will slay all the firstborn in the land of Egypt, from man to beast, and upon all the gods of Egypt I will perform acts of judgment, I, God."[47]

"I will pass through the land of Egypt on this night"—I and not an angel.

"I will slay all the firstborn in the land of Egypt"—I and not a seraph.

"Upon all the gods of Egypt I will perform acts of judgment"—I and not a messenger.

"I, God"—It is I, and none other!

"With a strong hand"—This refers to the pestilence, as the verse states: "Behold, the hand of God will place a very severe

"וְעָבַרְתִּי בְאֶרֶץ־מִצְרַיִם בַּלַּיְלָה הַזֶּה, וְהִכֵּיתִי כָל־בְּכוֹר בְּאֶרֶץ מִצְרַיִם מֵאָדָם וְעַד־בְּהֵמָה, וּבְכָל־אֱלֹהֵי מִצְרַיִם אֶעֱשֶׂה שְׁפָטִים, אֲנִי יְהוָה":

"וְעָבַרְתִּי בְאֶרֶץ־מִצְרַיִם בַּלַּיְלָה הַזֶּה" – אֲנִי וְלֹא מַלְאָךְ.

"וְהִכֵּיתִי כָל־בְּכוֹר בְּאֶרֶץ מִצְרַיִם" – אֲנִי וְלֹא שָׂרָף.

"וּבְכָל־אֱלֹהֵי מִצְרַיִם אֶעֱשֶׂה שְׁפָטִים" – אֲנִי וְלֹא הַשָּׁלִיחַ.

"אֲנִי יְהוָה" – אֲנִי הוּא וְלֹא אַחֵר:

"בְּיָד חֲזָקָה" – זוֹ הַדֶּבֶר – כְּמָה שֶׁנֶּאֱמַר: "הִנֵּה יַד־יְהוָה הוֹיָה בְּמִקְנְךָ אֲשֶׁר

Negative Example

There are those of us who are upset by the reading of the plagues. We are aware of the cruelty of the Egyptians. At the same time, it is difficult for us to read about such calamities as the plagues befalling any people. But there is a reason why these details were included in the Haggadah.

Up to this point, we've been speaking about the story of our slavery in Egypt from our own perspective. We've discussed our powerlessness as slaves and what God did for us when we surrendered to him. But there is a parallel "story within the story"—the Egyptian perspective.

Pharaoh and his people also experienced a story of addiction. However, their story does not end well for them. Pharaoh, in

בַּשָּׂדֶה בַּסוּסִים בַּחֲמֹרִים בַּגְּמַלִּים בַּבָּקָר וּבַצֹּאן, דֶּבֶר כָּבֵד מְאֹד":

"וּבִזְרֹעַ נְטוּיָה" — זוֹ הַחֶרֶב — כְּמָה שֶׁנֶּאֱמַר: "וְחַרְבּוֹ שְׁלוּפָה בְּיָדוֹ נְטוּיָה עַל יְרוּשָׁלָיִם":

"וּבְמֹרָא גָּדֹל" — זוֹ גִּלּוּי שְׁכִינָה — כְּמָה שֶׁנֶּאֱמַר: "אוֹ הֲנִסָּה אֱלֹהִים לָבֹא לָקַחַת לוֹ גוֹי מִקֶּרֶב גּוֹי, בְּמַסֹּת בְּאֹתֹת וּבְמוֹפְתִים וּבְמִלְחָמָה וּבְיָד חֲזָקָה וּבִזְרוֹעַ נְטוּיָה וּבְמוֹרָאִים גְּדֹלִים, כְּכֹל אֲשֶׁר־עָשָׂה לָכֶם יְהוָה אֱלֹהֵיכֶם בְּמִצְרַיִם לְעֵינֶיךָ":

pestilence upon your livestock in the field—upon the horses, the donkeys, the camels, the cattle, and the sheep."[48]

"With an outstretched arm"— this refers to the sword, as the verse states: "His sword drawn in His hand, stretched out over Jerusalem."[49]

"With great awe"— "great awe" referring to the revelation of the Shechinah (Divine Presence)—as the verse states: "Or has any deity performed miracles, coming to a nation and taking it for Himself out from another nation, with signs and wonders; with a war, a strong hand, an outstretched arm, and with awesome acts—like everything that God, your God, did for you in Egypt, before your eyes?"[50]

his arrogance, refused to ever acknowledge hitting bottom.

He brought himself and his entire nation to the point of devastation.

We do not gloat over the plagues that were brought upon Egypt. At the same time, it is important for us to bear witness to the inevitable outcome of self-will run riot.

The plagues suffered by Egypt remind us of the inevitable wreckage in the life of the unrecovered addict. As we remember what happened to the Egyptians, we are doubly thankful to God for our redemption.

There but for the grace of God go we. ♦

MAGGID

"וּבְאֹתוֹת" — זֶה הַמַּטֶּה — כְּמָה שֶׁנֶּאֱמַר: "וְאֶת־הַמַּטֶּה הַזֶּה תִּקַּח בְּיָדְךָ אֲשֶׁר תַּעֲשֶׂה־בּוֹ אֶת־הָאֹתֹת":

"With signs"— This refers to the staff, as the verse states: "You shall take this staff in your hand, with which you will perform the signs."[51]

"וּבְמֹפְתִים" — זֶה הַדָּם — כְּמָה שֶׁנֶּאֱמַר: "וְנָתַתִּי מוֹפְתִים בַּשָּׁמַיִם וּבָאָרֶץ,

"With wonders"— This refers to the blood, as the verse states: "I will show wonders in heaven and on earth...

- When saying each of the words "Blood, fire, and pillars of smoke," remove wine (three times) from the cup (either with your finger or by spilling).

דָּם וָאֵשׁ וְתִימְרוֹת עָשָׁן":

Blood, fire, and pillars of smoke."[52]

דָּבָר אַחֵר:
"בְּיָד חֲזָקָה" — שְׁתַּיִם.
"וּבִזְרֹעַ נְטוּיָה" — שְׁתַּיִם.
"וּבְמֹרָא גָּדֹל" — שְׁתַּיִם.
"וּבְאֹתוֹת" — שְׁתַּיִם.
"וּבְמֹפְתִים" — שְׁתַּיִם:

Another explanation:
"With a strong hand"— suggests two plagues;
"With an outstretched arm"— another two;
"With great awe"— another two;
"With signs"— another two;
"With wonders"— another two.

These are the Ten Plagues the Holy One, blessed be He, brought upon the Egyptians in Egypt. They are:

אֵלּוּ עֶשֶׂר מַכּוֹת שֶׁהֵבִיא הַקָּדוֹשׁ בָּרוּךְ הוּא עַל הַמִּצְרִים בְּמִצְרַיִם. וְאֵלּוּ הֵן:

- When saying the ten plagues remove the wine as before, ten times.

דָּם. צְפַרְדֵּעַ. כִּנִּים. עָרוֹב. דֶּבֶר. שְׁחִין. בָּרָד. אַרְבֶּה. חֹשֶׁךְ. מַכַּת בְּכוֹרוֹת:

Blood · Frogs · Lice · Wild Creatures Pestilence · Boils · Hail · Locusts · Darkness Slaying of the Firstborn.

Double Standard

Our tradition tells us that the hail that fell during the plagues was miraculous in that the ice pellets contained fire within.[53] We know that God does not perform a miracle for naught, so why did the hail have to miraculously contain fire?

The answer will be understood by explaining the principle of God's justice being meted out "measure for measure." Not only does the punishment fit the crime, but the punishment is an outer manifestation of the crime itself. Therefore, if we understand what Pharaoh and the Egyptians were being punished for, we will understand why it is so fitting that they were struck by hail that contained fire.

Pharaoh is the epitome of ego. It was his arrogance that did not allow him to admit defeat and release his slaves. He insisted on destroying his entire country rather than letting go. One of the most distinctive qualities of "self-will run riot" is a strange paradox. The self-obsessed person is simultaneously oblivious to the pain of others while hypersensitive to any injury—real or imagined—inflicted on him.

The egotistical person is thus cold on the outside and hot on the inside. That is to say, numb to other people's pain and

- When saying the words "Detzach Adash Be'achav" remove wine again three times.

Rabbi Yehudah would refer to them with a mnemonic:

רַבִּי יְהוּדָה הָיָה נוֹתֵן בָּהֶם סִמָּנִים:

דְּצַ"ךְ. עֲדַ"שׁ. בְּאַחַ"ב:
Detzach · Adash · Be'achav

- Now refill the cup with fresh wine (and dispose of the spilled wine).

acutely aware of his own. Pharaoh was thus punished measure for measure with miraculous hail that was cold ice on the outside and hot fire on the inside.[54]

In recovery we endeavor to completely reverse this double standard. The rule is: "We must be hard on ourselves and always considerate of others."

Short and Sweet

The Talmud[55] tells us that Rabbi Yehudah was honored with being the head speaker in every assembly of the Sages. One explanation as to why Rabbi Yehudah was a favored speaker was because of his ability to condense ideas into a brief format as exemplified by his shortening the ten plagues into an acronym.[56]

In recovery, we have found great value in the ability to keep things simple and convey great truths in brief, down-to-earth language. Dr. Bob, one of the cofounders of AA, once said that the entire Twelve-Step program could be succinctly summed up in six words: trust God, clean house, help others.

רַבִּי יוֹסֵי הַגְּלִילִי אוֹמֵר:

מִנַּיִן אַתָּה אוֹמֵר שֶׁלָּקוּ הַמִּצְרִים בְּמִצְרַיִם עֶשֶׂר מַכּוֹת וְעַל הַיָּם לָקוּ חֲמִשִּׁים מַכּוֹת? בְּמִצְרַיִם מָה הוּא אוֹמֵר: "וַיֹּאמְרוּ הַחַרְטֻמִּים אֶל־פַּרְעֹה אֶצְבַּע אֱלֹהִים הִיא."
וְעַל הַיָּם מָה הוּא אוֹמֵר: "וַיַּרְא יִשְׂרָאֵל אֶת־הַיָּד הַגְּדוֹלָה אֲשֶׁר עָשָׂה יְהוָה בְּמִצְרַיִם וַיִּירְאוּ הָעָם אֶת־יְהוָה וַיַּאֲמִינוּ בַּיהוָה וּבְמֹשֶׁה עַבְדּוֹ":
כַּמָּה לָקוּ בְאֶצְבַּע? עֶשֶׂר מַכּוֹת. אֱמוֹר מֵעַתָּה: בְּמִצְרַיִם לָקוּ עֶשֶׂר מַכּוֹת, וְעַל הַיָּם לָקוּ חֲמִשִּׁים מַכּוֹת:

Rabbi Yose Haglili says:

From where do you derive that the Egyptians were struck by ten plagues in Egypt, and were struck by fifty plagues at the sea? Concerning the plagues in Egypt the verse states: "The sorcerers said to Pharaoh, 'It is the finger of God.'"[57]
And concerning the plagues at the sea the verse states, "Israel saw the great hand God had enacted on the Egyptians, and the people feared God. They believed in God and in Moses, His servant."[58]
With how many plagues were they struck by the "finger" [in Egypt]? Ten plagues.
So you must now say that since in Egypt they were struck by ten plagues [from a single "finger"], at the sea they must have been struck by fifty plagues [from a whole "hand"]!

רַבִּי אֱלִיעֶזֶר אוֹמֵר:

מִנַּיִן שֶׁכָּל־מַכָּה וּמַכָּה שֶׁהֵבִיא הַקָּדוֹשׁ בָּרוּךְ הוּא עַל הַמִּצְרִים בְּמִצְרַיִם הָיְתָה שֶׁל אַרְבַּע מַכּוֹת? שֶׁנֶּאֱמַר: "יְשַׁלַּח־בָּם חֲרוֹן אַפּוֹ עֶבְרָה וָזַעַם

Rabbi Eliezer says:

From where do you derive that each plague the Holy One, blessed be He, brought upon the Egyptians in Egypt [and at the sea] consisted of four plagues?
From the verse: "He sent forth against them His fierce anger: fury, indignation, and misfortune, a band of messengers of evil."[59]

"Fury" is one;
"indignation" makes two;
"misfortune" makes three;
"a band of messengers of evil" makes four.
So you must now say that in Egypt they were struck by forty plagues [from a single "finger"], and at the sea they were struck by two hundred plagues [from a whole "hand"]!

Rabbi Akiva says:

From where do you derive that each plague the Holy One, blessed be He, brought upon the Egyptians in Egypt [and at the sea] consisted of five plagues? From the verse: "He sent forth against them his fierce anger, fury, indignation, and misfortune, a band of messengers of evil":
"His fierce anger" is one;
"fury" makes two;
"indignation" makes three;
"misfortune" makes four;
"a band of messengers of evil" makes five.
So you must now say that in Egypt they were struck by fifty plagues [from a single "finger"], and at the sea they were struck by two hundred and fifty plagues [from a whole "hand"]!

וְצָרָה מִשְׁלַחַת מַלְאֲכֵי רָעִים":
"עֶבְרָה" — אַחַת.
"וָזַעַם" — שְׁתַּיִם.
"וְצָרָה" — שָׁלֹשׁ.
"מִשְׁלַחַת מַלְאֲכֵי רָעִים" — אַרְבַּע.
אֱמוֹר מֵעַתָּה: בְּמִצְרַיִם לָקוּ אַרְבָּעִים מַכּוֹת, וְעַל הַיָּם לָקוּ מָאתַיִם מַכּוֹת:

רַבִּי עֲקִיבָא אוֹמֵר:

מִנַּיִן שֶׁכָּל־מַכָּה וּמַכָּה שֶׁהֵבִיא הַקָּדוֹשׁ בָּרוּךְ הוּא עַל הַמִּצְרִים בְּמִצְרַיִם הָיְתָה שֶׁל חָמֵשׁ מַכּוֹת? שֶׁנֶּאֱמַר: "יְשַׁלַּח־בָּם חֲרוֹן אַפּוֹ עֶבְרָה וָזַעַם וְצָרָה מִשְׁלַחַת מַלְאֲכֵי רָעִים":
"חֲרוֹן אַפּוֹ" — אַחַת.
"עֶבְרָה" — שְׁתַּיִם.
"וָזַעַם" — שָׁלֹשׁ.
"וְצָרָה" — אַרְבַּע.
"מִשְׁלַחַת מַלְאֲכֵי רָעִים" — חָמֵשׁ.
אֱמוֹר מֵעַתָּה: בְּמִצְרַיִם לָקוּ חֲמִשִּׁים מַכּוֹת, וְעַל הַיָּם לָקוּ חֲמִשִּׁים וּמָאתַיִם מַכּוֹת:

מַגִּיד

כַּמָּה מַעֲלוֹת טוֹבוֹת לַמָּקוֹם עָלֵינוּ!

How many are the good things that the Almighty has showered upon us!

Never Enough

It seems like a contradiction that we say Dayeinu ("it would have been enough for us") after listing each of the miracles God did for us, but then we continue to list more and more miracles. If it was enough, why does the list continue? Conversely, if the list continues, clearly it was not enough.

The answer to this question can be found upon closer examination of the exact words used. The term Dayeinu means "it would have been enough for *us*." *We* would have been satisfied.

Clearly, however, God was not yet satisfied, and He continued to bring us to greater levels of freedom.

Many of us came to recovery with certain goals in mind. For many of us it was as simple as putting a pause to the chaos and destruction in our lives. When these goals are met, it is easy to become satisfied and declare, "Dayeinu! It is enough for us."

We must remember that while we may have come to recovery for our own reasons, as we begin to experience a spiritual awakening, we realize that we are no longer here for our own purpose. We are here to serve God, and, indeed, our sobriety belongs to Him.

So even when we find ourselves in a comfortable place, even when our lives are better than we could have dreamed, God may very well still have more in store for us.

Dayeinu—it would have been enough for *us*. But it was not enough for the infinite God. ♦

אִלּוּ הוֹצִיאָנוּ מִמִּצְרַיִם וְלֹא עָשָׂה בָּהֶם שְׁפָטִים דַּיֵּנוּ:
If He had brought us out of Egypt,
but had not carried out judgments against them
—it would have been enough for us!

אִלּוּ עָשָׂה בָּהֶם שְׁפָטִים וְלֹא עָשָׂה בֵאלֹהֵיהֶם דַּיֵּנוּ:
If He had carried out judgments against them,
but not against their gods
—it would have been enough for us!

אִלּוּ עָשָׂה בֵאלֹהֵיהֶם וְלֹא הָרַג אֶת־בְּכוֹרֵיהֶם דַּיֵּנוּ:
If He had destroyed their gods, but had not slain their firstborn
—it would have been enough for us!

אִלּוּ הָרַג אֶת־בְּכוֹרֵיהֶם וְלֹא נָתַן לָנוּ אֶת־מָמוֹנָם דַּיֵּנוּ:
If He had slain their firstborn, but had not given us their wealth
—it would have been enough for us!

Revealing Our Inner Potential

The Splitting of the Sea is one of the most emblematic miracles in our people's miraculous history; yet, it is also one of the most misunderstood.

If the purpose of splitting the sea was merely so the Jewish people could escape the oncoming Egyptian armies, there are so many other ways that God could have saved them. Why did God specifically choose to split the sea? (God doesn't do a miracle for naught.)[60]

Kabbalistic teachings explain that the dry land and the sea are symbolic of the material world and the spiritual world, respectively.[61] Everything on dry land is readily apparent to us—just as the material world is easy to see. That which is submerged beneath the water is hidden from our view—just as spiritual reality cannot be seen with our physical eyes.

The Splitting of the Sea therefore represents removing the cover that obscures our view of spirituality, allowing us to see

דַּיֵּנוּ

אִלּוּ נָתַן לָנוּ אֶת־מָמוֹנָם וְלֹא קָרַע לָנוּ אֶת־הַיָּם דַּיֵּנוּ:
If He had given us their wealth, but had not split the sea for us
—it would have been enough for us!

אִלּוּ קָרַע לָנוּ אֶת־הַיָּם וְלֹא הֶעֱבִירָנוּ בְּתוֹכוֹ בֶּחָרָבָה דַּיֵּנוּ:
If He had split the sea for us,
but had not led us through it on dry land
—it would have been enough for us!

אִלּוּ הֶעֱבִירָנוּ בְּתוֹכוֹ בֶּחָרָבָה וְלֹא שִׁקַּע צָרֵינוּ בְּתוֹכוֹ דַּיֵּנוּ:
If He had taken us through it on dry land,
but had not drowned our oppressors in it
—it would have been enough for us!

---

the hidden spiritual truths as clearly as we are normally able to see the material.

It's important for us to realize that the Exodus was not merely a process by which we gained freedom from our masters. It was also, and perhaps even more so, a process through which we uncovered our true potential and finally encountered our true selves.

Each of us experiences "sea-splitting moments," where the spirituality that was concealed deeply within is suddenly revealed and is as plain to see as the physical. Indeed, we might say that this revelation of our deepest self is the entire point of the enslavement and ensuing Exodus. If we would have merely left our taskmasters and gained freedom without uncovering the deepest spiritual truths within ourselves, our exodus would be profoundly lacking.

In simple terms that we can relate to, this means that recovery is about so much more than just the freedom from drugs, alcohol, and other destructive behaviors. Recovery is about revealing inner spiritual powers that had been hidden within and would otherwise have never become known to ourselves.

MAGGID

**אִלּוּ שִׁקַּע צָרֵינוּ בְּתוֹכוֹ
וְלֹא סִפֵּק צָרְכֵּנוּ בַּמִּדְבָּר אַרְבָּעִים שָׁנָה דַּיֵּנוּ:**

If He had drowned our oppressors in it,
but had not supplied our needs in the desert for forty years
—it would have been enough for us!

**אִלּוּ סִפֵּק צָרְכֵּנוּ בַּמִּדְבָּר אַרְבָּעִים שָׁנָה
וְלֹא הֶאֱכִילָנוּ אֶת־הַמָּן דַּיֵּנוּ:**

If He had supplied our needs in the desert for forty years,
but had not fed us the Manna
—it would have been enough for us!

אִלּוּ הֶאֱכִילָנוּ אֶת־הַמָּן וְלֹא נָתַן לָנוּ אֶת־הַשַּׁבָּת דַּיֵּנוּ:

If He had fed us the Manna, but had not given us the Shabbos
—it would have been enough for us!

אִלּוּ נָתַן לָנוּ אֶת־הַשַּׁבָּת וְלֹא קֵרְבָנוּ לִפְנֵי הַר־סִינַי דַּיֵּנוּ:

If He had given us the Shabbos,
but had not brought us before Mount Sinai
—it would have been enough for us!

אִלּוּ קֵרְבָנוּ לִפְנֵי הַר־סִינַי וְלֹא נָתַן לָנוּ אֶת־הַתּוֹרָה דַּיֵּנוּ:

If He had brought us before Mount Sinai,
but had not given us the Torah
—it would have been enough for us!

אִלּוּ נָתַן לָנוּ אֶת־הַתּוֹרָה וְלֹא הִכְנִיסָנוּ לְאֶרֶץ יִשְׂרָאֵל דַּיֵּנוּ:

If He had given us the Torah,
but had not brought us into the Land of Israel
—it would have been enough for us!

אִלּוּ הִכְנִיסָנוּ לְאֶרֶץ יִשְׂרָאֵל וְלֹא בָנָה לָנוּ אֶת־בֵּית הַבְּחִירָה דַּיֵּנוּ:

If He had brought us into the Land of Israel,
but had not built for us the Chosen House
—it would have been enough for us!

עַל אַחַת כַּמָּה וְכַמָּה
How much more so

טוֹבָה כְפוּלָה וּמְכֻפֶּלֶת לַמָּקוֹם עָלֵינוּ.	should we be grateful to God for the doubled and redoubled goodness that He has bestowed upon us!
שֶׁהוֹצִיאָנוּ מִמִּצְרַיִם.	He brought us out of Egypt;
וְעָשָׂה בָהֶם שְׁפָטִים.	and He carried out judgments against them;
וְעָשָׂה בֵאלֹהֵיהֶם.	and against their gods;
וְהָרַג אֶת־בְּכוֹרֵיהֶם.	and He slayed their firstborn;
וְנָתַן לָנוּ אֶת־מָמוֹנָם.	and He gave us their wealth;
וְקָרַע לָנוּ אֶת־הַיָּם.	and He split the sea for us;
וְהֶעֱבִירָנוּ בְתוֹכוֹ בֶּחָרָבָה.	and He led us through it on dry land;
וְשִׁקַּע צָרֵינוּ בְּתוֹכוֹ.	and He drowned our oppressors in it;
וְסִפֵּק צָרְכֵּנוּ בַּמִּדְבָּר אַרְבָּעִים שָׁנָה.	and He supplied our needs in the desert for forty years;
וְהֶאֱכִילָנוּ אֶת־הַמָּן.	and He fed us the Manna;
וְנָתַן לָנוּ אֶת־הַשַּׁבָּת.	and He gave us the Shabbos;
וְקֵרְבָנוּ לִפְנֵי הַר־סִינַי.	and He brought us before Mount Sinai;
וְנָתַן לָנוּ אֶת־הַתּוֹרָה.	and He gave us the Torah;
וְהִכְנִיסָנוּ לְאֶרֶץ יִשְׂרָאֵל.	and He brought us into the Land of Israel;
וּבָנָה לָנוּ אֶת־בֵּית הַבְּחִירָה לְכַפֵּר עַל כָּל־עֲוֹנוֹתֵינוּ:	and He built the Chosen House for us, to atone for all our sins.

MAGGID

רַבָּן גַּמְלִיאֵל הָיָה אוֹמֵר: כָּל־שֶׁלֹּא אָמַר שְׁלֹשָׁה דְבָרִים אֵלּוּ בַּפֶּסַח לֹא יָצָא יְדֵי חוֹבָתוֹ. וְאֵלּוּ הֵן:

Rabban Gamliel used to say: "Whoever has not mentioned the following three things on Pesach has not fulfilled his obligation. They are:

פֶּסַח מַצָּה וּמָרוֹר
Pesach, Matzah, and Maror."

פֶּסַח שֶׁהָיוּ אֲבוֹתֵינוּ אוֹכְלִים בִּזְמַן שֶׁבֵּית הַמִּקְדָּשׁ קַיָּם עַל־שׁוּם מָה? עַל־שׁוּם שֶׁפָּסַח הַקָּדוֹשׁ בָּרוּךְ הוּא עַל־בָּתֵּי אֲבוֹתֵינוּ בְּמִצְרַיִם. שֶׁנֶּאֱמַר: "וַאֲמַרְתֶּם זֶבַח־פֶּסַח הוּא לַיהוָה אֲשֶׁר פָּסַח עַל־בָּתֵּי בְנֵי־יִשְׂרָאֵל בְּמִצְרַיִם בְּנָגְפּוֹ אֶת־מִצְרַיִם וְאֶת־בָּתֵּינוּ הִצִּיל, וַיִּקֹּד הָעָם וַיִּשְׁתַּחֲווּ:"

Pesach—The Paschal lamb that our ancestors ate when the Holy Temple stood—is for what reason? Because God passed over our forebears' houses in Egypt, as the verse states: "You should say, 'It is a Pesach-offering to God, because He passed over the houses of the Children of Israel in Egypt when He struck the Egyptians, and He spared our households.' Then the people bowed down and prostrated themselves."[62]

- The middle Matzah is lifted up and shown while the following passage is recited.

This Matzah—

unleavened bread—that we eat is for what reason? Because the dough of our ancestors did not have time to become leavened before the King—the King of kings, the Holy One, blessed be He—revealed Himself to them and redeemed them, as the verse states: "They baked the dough that they had taken out of Egypt into cakes of Matzos, for it had not leavened, since they were driven out of Egypt and could not delay, but had also not prepared any provisions."[63]

מַצָּה זוֹ שֶׁאָנוּ אוֹכְלִים עַל־שׁוּם מָה? עַל־שׁוּם שֶׁלֹּא הִסְפִּיק בְּצֵקָם שֶׁל אֲבוֹתֵינוּ לְהַחֲמִיץ עַד שֶׁנִּגְלָה עֲלֵיהֶם מֶלֶךְ מַלְכֵי הַמְּלָכִים הַקָּדוֹשׁ בָּרוּךְ הוּא וּגְאָלָם. שֶׁנֶּאֱמַר: "וַיֹּאפוּ אֶת־הַבָּצֵק אֲשֶׁר הוֹצִיאוּ מִמִּצְרַיִם עֻגֹת מַצּוֹת, כִּי לֹא חָמֵץ, כִּי־גֹרְשׁוּ מִמִּצְרַיִם וְלֹא יָכְלוּ לְהִתְמַהְמֵהַּ וְגַם־צֵדָה לֹא־עָשׂוּ לָהֶם":

Ready Or Not

Why did we eat flat unleavened bread while leaving Egypt? We are told the reason is that our dough did not have time to rise.

Think about this for a moment: We were in exile in Egypt for two hundred and ten years. The process of the ten plagues took a year. How is it possible that we were so ill-prepared for the Exodus that we did not even have food ready?

But that is precisely the point. When the moment of redemption arrives, it does so suddenly. It is not on our schedule; it is on God's schedule. As the Haggadah says, "The dough of our ancestors did not have time to become leavened before the King—the King of kings, the Holy One, blessed be He—revealed Himself to them and redeemed them."

No matter how long we are enslaved or how long we've been trying to escape our slavery—when the moment of redemption finally arrives, we realize that it is a power far greater than ourselves that is being revealed. In other words, the redemption did not come about because of human effort.

- The bitter herbs are lifted up and shown while the following passage is recited.

This Maror—bitter herbs—that we eat is for what reason? Because the Egyptians embittered our ancestors' lives in Egypt, as the verse states: "And they embittered their lives with hard labor, with mortar and with bricks and with all kinds of labor in the field, all their work that they made them do was crushing labor."[64]

מָרוֹר זֶה שֶׁאָנוּ אוֹכְלִים עַל־שׁוּם מָה? עַל שׁוּם שֶׁמֵּרְרוּ הַמִּצְרִים אֶת־חַיֵּי אֲבוֹתֵינוּ בְּמִצְרָיִם. שֶׁנֶּאֱמַר: "וַיְמָרְרוּ אֶת־חַיֵּיהֶם בַּעֲבֹדָה קָשָׁה בְּחֹמֶר וּבִלְבֵנִים וּבְכָל־עֲבֹדָה בַּשָּׂדֶה, אֵת כָּל־עֲבֹדָתָם אֲשֶׁר־עָבְדוּ בָהֶם בְּפָרֶךְ":

If it did, then we would have been ready for it when it happened. Rather, redemption is something that happened *to* us, and our only response was to surrender to it and allow it to happen.

We know the importance of patience and that "time takes time"; however, there is an opposite lesson as well: When God suddenly reveals Himself, we do not drag our heels and prolong the process. We do not insist that our bread isn't ready and that we need more time to prepare. Rather, we humbly accept the fact that something is happening to us that we could never have done for ourselves and that we need to surrender to God's plan and allow it to take us where He wants us to go.

מַצָּה

בְּכָל־דּוֹר וָדוֹר
חַיָּב אָדָם לִרְאוֹת אֶת־עַצְמוֹ כְּאִלּוּ הוּא יָצָא מִמִּצְרַיִם. שֶׁנֶּאֱמַר:

In each and every generation,
a person must see themselves as if they had personally left Egypt, as the verse states:

Exodus after Exodus

What does it mean when it says, "In each and every generation a person must see themself as if they had personally left Egypt"?

The *Big Book* says, "It is easy to let up on the spiritual program of action and rest on our laurels. We are headed for trouble if we do…."

The Exodus from Egypt is not just something that happened in the past, it is something that continues happening on ever higher levels.

The Torah says,[65] "These are the journeys of the Jewish people leaving Egypt." It seems odd that the Torah would refer to multiple journeys out of Egypt. Although the Jewish people took forty-two journeys during the forty years of traveling from Egypt to the Promised Land, there was only one actual jaunt from within Egypt to over the border and into the wilderness.[66] In other words, there was only one trip that actually took the Jewish people out of Egypt; the other forty-one trips all took place outside of Egypt. Why, then, does the Torah say, "These are the journeys (plural) out of Egypt"?

One explanation is that Egypt is a relative term. The Biblical name for Egypt is "Mitzrayim," which is related to the word Meitzarim, meaning "strictures" or "narrow places." Today's "Promised Land" can easily become tomorrow's "Egypt." In that sense, we must never stop leaving Egypt.

We know in recovery that "we cannot rest on our laurels." We know about the danger of "one who fails to maintain and enlarge his spiritual condition." We are grateful for the exodus we have experienced, and we are eager to experience a new exodus every day.

"וְהִגַּדְתָּ לְבִנְךָ בַּיּוֹם הַהוּא לֵאמֹר, בַּעֲבוּר זֶה עָשָׂה יְהֹוָה לִי בְּצֵאתִי מִמִּצְרָיִם": לֹא אֶת־אֲבוֹתֵינוּ בִּלְבַד גָּאַל הַקָּדוֹשׁ בָּרוּךְ הוּא אֶלָּא אַף אוֹתָנוּ גָּאַל עִמָּהֶם. שֶׁנֶּאֱמַר: "וְאוֹתָנוּ הוֹצִיא מִשָּׁם, לְמַעַן הָבִיא אוֹתָנוּ לָתֶת לָנוּ אֶת־הָאָרֶץ אֲשֶׁר נִשְׁבַּע לַאֲבוֹתֵינוּ":

"You shall tell your child on that day, saying, 'It is because of this that God did for me when I left Egypt.'"[67] It was not only our ancestors whom the Holy One, blessed be He, redeemed, but He redeemed us with them too, as the verse states: "He brought us out from there to bring us to the land that He swore to our ancestors and gave it to us."[68]

Bearing Witness

You may have noticed that in this commentary we interchangeably speak about the Exodus as a historical event that happened long ago and as a personal experience that is happening to each of us. This is the meaning of the words "In every generation."

When we tell the story of the Exodus, we are not commemorating or even reenacting something that happened to other people. We are living it right now. The Exodus is happening now. Every attendee at the Seder is obligated to feel this.

For those of us who have experienced the miracles of recovery, we are grateful that it is easier to attain that mindset. At this point we encourage you to speak up and tell those with whom you are seated right now that you can personally attest to the fact that the Exodus is something that has happened in your lifetime and is even happening right now.

- Cover the Matzos and hold the cup in your right hand.

Therefore

לְפִיכָךְ

it is our duty to thank, praise, extol, glorify, exalt, honor, bless, ennoble, and acclaim He Who did all these miracles for our ancestors and for us.

אֲנַחְנוּ חַיָּבִים לְהוֹדוֹת לְהַלֵּל לְשַׁבֵּחַ לְפָאֵר לְרוֹמֵם לְהַדֵּר לְבָרֵךְ לְעַלֵּה וּלְקַלֵּס. לְמִי שֶׁעָשָׂה לַאֲבוֹתֵינוּ וְלָנוּ אֶת־כָּל־הַנִּסִּים הָאֵלּוּ.

He took us out from slavery to freedom, from grief to joyousness, and from mourning to festivity, and from darkness to bright light, and from bondage to redemption. So let us declare before Him a new song, Halleluyah!

הוֹצִיאָנוּ מֵעַבְדוּת לְחֵרוּת. מִיָּגוֹן לְשִׂמְחָה. וּמֵאֵבֶל לְיוֹם טוֹב. וּמֵאֲפֵלָה לְאוֹר גָּדוֹל. וּמִשִּׁעְבּוּד לִגְאֻלָּה. וְנֹאמַר לְפָנָיו שִׁירָה חֲדָשָׁה הַלְלוּיָהּ:

- (Some put the cup down on the table.)

Halleluyah!

הַלְלוּיָהּ

Give praise, you servants of God! Praise the name of God! May God's name be blessed from now and forever. From the rising of the sun to its setting, God's name is praised. High above all nations is God, His glory is above the heavens. Who is like God, our God, Who is enthroned on high yet looks down low upon heaven and earth? He raises the poor from the dust; from the trash heaps He lifts the needy, to seat them with nobles, with the nobles

הַלְלוּ עַבְדֵי יְהֹוָה, הַלְלוּ אֶת־שֵׁם יְהֹוָה: יְהִי שֵׁם יְהֹוָה מְבֹרָךְ, מֵעַתָּה וְעַד־עוֹלָם: מִמִּזְרַח־שֶׁמֶשׁ עַד־מְבוֹאוֹ, מְהֻלָּל שֵׁם יְהֹוָה: רָם עַל־כָּל־גּוֹיִם | יְהֹוָה, עַל הַשָּׁמַיִם כְּבוֹדוֹ: מִי כַּיהֹוָה אֱלֹהֵינוּ, הַמַּגְבִּיהִי לָשָׁבֶת: הַמַּשְׁפִּילִי לִרְאוֹת, בַּשָּׁמַיִם וּבָאָרֶץ: מְקִימִי מֵעָפָר דָּל, מֵאַשְׁפֹּת יָרִים אֶבְיוֹן: לְהוֹשִׁיבִי עִם־נְדִיבִים, עִם נְדִיבֵי עַמּוֹ:

MAGGID

of His people. He transforms the barren wife into a joyful mother of children. Halleluyah!

מוֹשִׁיבִי עֲקֶרֶת הַבַּיִת אֵם־הַבָּנִים שְׂמֵחָה, הַלְלוּיָהּ:

When Israel went out of Egypt, the House of Jacob from a people of foreign tongue, Judah became His sanctuary, Israel His dominions. The sea saw and fled; the Jordan turned backward. The mountains skipped like rams, the hills like young lambs. What is with you, O sea, that you flee? O Jordan, that you turn backward? O mountains, that you skip like rams? O hills, like young lambs? Before the Master, Who formed the earth. Before the God of Jacob, Who turns rock into a pond of water, the flint into a fountain of water.

בְּצֵאת יִשְׂרָאֵל מִמִּצְרָיִם, בֵּית יַעֲקֹב מֵעַם לֹעֵז: הָיְתָה יְהוּדָה לְקָדְשׁוֹ, יִשְׂרָאֵל מַמְשְׁלוֹתָיו: הַיָּם רָאָה וַיָּנֹס, הַיַּרְדֵּן יִסֹּב לְאָחוֹר: הֶהָרִים רָקְדוּ כְאֵילִים, גְּבָעוֹת כִּבְנֵי־צֹאן: מַה־לְּךָ הַיָּם כִּי תָנוּס, הַיַּרְדֵּן תִּסֹּב לְאָחוֹר: הֶהָרִים תִּרְקְדוּ כְאֵילִים, גְּבָעוֹת כִּבְנֵי־צֹאן: מִלִּפְנֵי אָדוֹן חוּלִי אָרֶץ, מִלִּפְנֵי אֱלֹוהַּ יַעֲקֹב: הַהֹפְכִי הַצּוּר אֲגַם־מָיִם, חַלָּמִישׁ לְמַעְיְנוֹ־מָיִם:

- All hold the cup at this point.

Blessed are You, God, our God, King of the universe, Who has redeemed us and redeemed our ancestors from Egypt, and brought us to this night to eat Matzah and Maror. Likewise, God, our God and God of our ancestors, bring us to other high holidays and festivals that will come to us in peace, gladdened

בָּרוּךְ אַתָּה יְהֹוָה אֱלֹהֵינוּ מֶלֶךְ הָעוֹלָם, אֲשֶׁר גְּאָלָנוּ וְגָאַל אֶת־אֲבוֹתֵינוּ מִמִּצְרַיִם וְהִגִּיעָנוּ הַלַּיְלָה הַזֶּה לֶאֱכָל־בּוֹ מַצָּה וּמָרוֹר. כֵּן יְהֹוָה אֱלֹהֵינוּ וֵאלֹהֵי אֲבוֹתֵינוּ יַגִּיעֵנוּ לְמוֹעֲדִים וְלִרְגָלִים אֲחֵרִים הַבָּאִים לִקְרָאתֵנוּ

מגיד

לְשָׁלוֹם שְׂמֵחִים בְּבִנְיַן עִירֶךָ וְשָׂשִׂים בַּעֲבוֹדָתֶךָ, וְנֹאכַל שָׁם מִן הַזְּבָחִים וּמִן הַפְּסָחִים
(on Saturday night -
מִן הַפְּסָחִים וּמִן הַזְּבָחִים)
אֲשֶׁר יַגִּיעַ דָּמָם עַל קִיר מִזְבַּחֲךָ לְרָצוֹן, וְנוֹדֶה לְךָ שִׁיר חָדָשׁ עַל גְּאֻלָּתֵנוּ וְעַל פְּדוּת נַפְשֵׁנוּ: בָּרוּךְ אַתָּה יְהֹוָה, גָּאַל יִשְׂרָאֵל:

in the rebuilding of Your city and joyful in Your service. Then we shall eat of the [Chagigah] sacrifices and of the Pesach offerings (on Saturday night—of the Pesach-offerings and of the [Chagigah] sacrifices [the next day]), whose blood will be sprinkled on the wall of Your altar for acceptance. We will then thank You with a new song for our redemption and for the liberation of our souls. Blessed are You, God, Who redeemed Israel.

בָּרוּךְ אַתָּה יְהֹוָה אֱלֹהֵינוּ מֶלֶךְ הָעוֹלָם, בּוֹרֵא פְּרִי הַגָּפֶן:

Blessed are You, God, our God, King of the universe, Who creates the fruit of the vine.

- Recline to the left and drink the entire cup (or at least the majority of it), preferably without pausing.

SEDER STEP 6
RACHTZAH

WASHING THE HANDS

- It is customary for the head of the household to have the water brought to their seat.
- With a cup, each person washes the right hand twice, and then washes the left hand twice.
- Make the following blessing:

בָּרוּךְ אַתָּה יְהֹוָה אֱלֹהֵינוּ מֶלֶךְ הָעוֹלָם, אֲשֶׁר קִדְּשָׁנוּ בְּמִצְוֹתָיו וְצִוָּנוּ עַל נְטִילַת יָדָיִם:

Blessed are You, God, our God, King of the universe, Who has sanctified us with His commandments and commanded us about the washing of the hands.

- Dry your hands and do not talk.

Always Ascending

We now wash our hands for the second time this evening—this time in preparation for the meal.

It has been pointed out that a deeper meaning of the second hand-washing is that in matters of self-cleansing and purification, we always rise higher and higher. Although we washed our hands not long ago, we wash our hands again. We experience higher and higher levels of making ourselves clean and pure before God.

 SEDER STEP 7
MOTZI

BLESSING BEFORE THE MEAL

- Hold the two whole Matzos and the broken piece in the middle with both hands and say:

בָּרוּךְ אַתָּה יְהֹוָה אֱלֹהֵינוּ מֶלֶךְ הָעוֹלָם, הַמּוֹצִיא לֶחֶם מִן הָאָרֶץ:

Blessed are You, God, our God, King of the universe, Who brings forth bread from the earth.

- Do not break the Matzah yet.

Into Action

So far, this evening, we have been performing the mitzvah of telling the story of our liberation. We are now about to perform the other major mitzvah of the night, which is eating the Matzah. We are reminded that words without action are not enough. As inspiring as the insights of the Haggadah are, this Seder is not complete until we actually consume the Matzah.

We don't just talk about Matzah, we eat it. It is a physical experience. At this point, whether we are ready or not, whether we have fully attained insights into its meaning or not, we take action. We get up from our seats, we wash our hands, we say the blessings, and we eat the required amount of Matzah.

To some this may seem overly technical. They may question the importance of such a seemingly mundane act as eating

SEDER STEP 8
MATZAH

MATZAH

- Let go of the bottom Matzah. Keep holding the top two.
- Say the following blessing, having in mind that it applies also to the Korech ("sandwich") and Afikoman:

בָּרוּךְ אַתָּה יְהֹוָה אֱלֹהֵינוּ מֶלֶךְ הָעוֹלָם, אֲשֶׁר קִדְּשָׁנוּ בְּמִצְוֹתָיו וְצִוָּנוּ עַל אֲכִילַת מַצָּה:

Blessed are You, God, our God, King of the universe, Who has sanctified us with His commandments and commanded us about eating Matzah.

- Take at least 0.9 oz. from each of the two Matzos that you are holding and eat them together.
- Eat all the Matzah within 2 minutes (or at most 9), while reclining to the left.
- Every adult must eat at least 1.5 oz. of Matzah.
- Most people do not dip this Matzah in salt.

a portion of Matzah. However, we understand very well the power of, and necessity for, simple action.

There is another powerful symbolism related to the fact that we are actually ingesting Matzah. Not only is this a physical act but it is one that causes a physical change in ourselves. The food we eat becomes part of our bodies. The lesson here is that ideas are all well and good, but we need to see physical, tangible results in our service of God. And that can only happen when we take physical action.

SEDER STEP 9
MAROR

BITTER HERBS

- All adults must eat 1.1 oz. (or at least 0.62 oz.) of Maror [grated horseradish and/or romaine lettuce].
- Dip the Maror into the Charoses.
- Say the following blessing, having in mind that it applies also to the bitter herbs in the Korech ("sandwich").

בָּרוּךְ אַתָּה יְהֹוָה אֱלֹהֵינוּ מֶלֶךְ הָעוֹלָם, אֲשֶׁר קִדְּשָׁנוּ בְּמִצְוֹתָיו וְצִוָּנוּ עַל אֲכִילַת מָרוֹר:

Blessed are You, God, our God, King of the universe, Who has sanctified us with His commandments and commanded us about eating Maror.

- Eat the entire amount within 2 minutes (or at most 9).
- Do not lean.

Maximum Impact

In the times of the Holy Temple, not only was there a mitzvah to eat the Matzah and the bitter herbs on this night, there was also a mitzvah to eat of the meat of the Passover Sacrifice. These are three different obligations.

The innovation of Hillel was to take all three of these mitzvah foods, bind them together, and eat them all at once.

There is a profound symbolism here. We are not satisfied to only do the next right thing. We want to do as many of the right things as we possibly can. Yes, in this way we are "selfish." We are eager to do as much as we can for our Maker and for others, never resting, never being content

SEDER STEP 10
KORECH

SANDWICH

- Take a piece from the third Matzah (1.1 oz., or at least 0.62 oz.) and the same amount of Maror (horseradish and/or romaine lettuce).
- Dip the bitter herbs in Charoses.
- Make a sandwich, and say the following:

זֵכֶר לְמִקְדָּשׁ כְּהִלֵּל. כֵּן עָשָׂה הִלֵּל בִּזְמַן שֶׁבֵּית הַמִּקְדָּשׁ הָיָה קַיָּם הָיָה כּוֹרֵךְ (פֶּסַח) מַצָּה וּמָרוֹר וְאוֹכֵל בְּיַחַד. לְקַיֵּם מַה שֶּׁנֶּאֱמַר: "עַל מַצּוֹת וּמְרוֹרִים יֹאכְלֻהוּ":

In remembrance of the Temple, we do as Hillel did at the time when the Holy Temple was standing: He would combine (Paschal lamb,) Matzah and Maror and eat them together, to fulfill the verse, "They shall eat it together with Matzos and Maror."[69]

- Eat the whole sandwich within 2 minutes (or at most 9), while reclining to the left.

when it comes to pursuing usefulness and service. Therefore, if there are multiple Mitzvos that can be packed into one bite, we do so with fervor.

As the *Big Book* asks us to consider during our daily reflections: Are we thinking only about ourselves? Or about "what we could pack into the stream of life"? 🍷

FESTIVE MEAL

- It is customary to begin by eating egg in salt water.
- Enjoy a good festive meal but leave some room for the Afikoman.
- Many have the custom not to bring any Matzah into contact with water.
- Some are careful to lean throughout the meal.

Never Give Up

The instructions for this step of the Seder are very simple—eat and drink as you please. This includes having more cups of wine or grape juice in addition to the four official cups that we drink tonight.

It is interesting to note that after Kiddush—the first cup—we don't drink again until the second cup. After the third cup, over which we recite the Grace After Meals, we don't drink again until the fourth cup. And after the fourth cup we don't drink again for the rest of the night. Only the second cup may be followed by as many other cups as you desire.

What can we learn from this?

Kabbalah tells us that the four children correspond to the four cups.[70] Accordingly, the second cup corresponds to the second child—the wicked child.

The lesson for us is that when it comes to speaking to the wicked child, who feels estranged from the entire Seder experience, we are enjoined to make as many attempts as necessary for them to hear our message. We are no strangers to the idea that carrying the message can be a lengthy process and that repeated attempts to do so are often necessary. As it says in the *Big Book*,[71] "Do not be discouraged if your prospect does not respond at once." We cannot force anyone to hear what they are not yet ready to hear, but we can be willing to tell our own story as many times as necessary when we think it may help.

SEDER STEP 12
TZAFUN

AFIKOMAN

- The Afikoman should be eaten before Halachic midnight.
- Everybody should eat a double portion of Matzah (a total of at least 1.24 oz.): one portion to remember the Paschal lamb and another portion to remember the Matzah eaten with the Paschal lamb.
- If this is too difficult, eat a single portion of Matzah (at least 0.62 oz.).
- Eat all the Matzah within 2 minutes (or at most 9), while reclining to the left.
- Do not eat or drink after eating the Afikoman (except water, etc.).

An Unusual Dessert

At the end of our festive meal, we consume Matzah once more, and it will be the last thing that we will eat this evening. We refer to this as the Afikoman. The word Afikoman comes from the Greek word for "dessert,"[72] but what kind of dessert is flat, tasteless Matzah?

The lesson to us is that after all is said and done, we need to constantly remember that "we realize we know only a little."[73] As we explained earlier regarding the answer to the wise son, the bland Matzah is a reminder to us to keep it simple and to accept that not everything has to be intellectually exciting or even make sense to us all the time. Therefore, we end our meal not with a flavorful dessert but with a reminder of our need to embrace simplicity.

Hold On to Humility

We also remember that the flat Matzah represents the deflation of ego. After everything we have been through tonight, all of the retelling of the glorious miracles and wonders, we do not become puffed up and arrogant. Rather, we end our meal with the same humility as we began it.

 **SEDER STEP 13**
BARECH

GRACE AFTER MEALS

- (According to some, Elijah's cup of wine is now poured.)
- The third cup of wine is poured.

A Song of Ascents.

שִׁיר הַמַּעֲלוֹת, בְּשׁוּב יְהֹוָה אֶת־שִׁיבַת צִיּוֹן, הָיִינוּ כְּחֹלְמִים: אָז יִמָּלֵא שְׂחוֹק פִּינוּ וּלְשׁוֹנֵנוּ רִנָּה, אָז יֹאמְרוּ בַגּוֹיִם הִגְדִּיל יְהֹוָה לַעֲשׂוֹת עִם־אֵלֶּה: הִגְדִּיל יְהֹוָה לַעֲשׂוֹת עִמָּנוּ, הָיִינוּ שְׂמֵחִים: שׁוּבָה יְהֹוָה אֶת־שְׁבִיתֵנוּ, כַּאֲפִיקִים בַּנֶּגֶב: הַזֹּרְעִים בְּדִמְעָה בְּרִנָּה יִקְצֹרוּ: הָלוֹךְ יֵלֵךְ וּבָכֹה נֹשֵׂא מֶשֶׁךְ־הַזָּרַע, בֹּא־יָבֹא בְרִנָּה נֹשֵׂא אֲלֻמֹּתָיו:

When God will return the exiles of Zion, we will be like dreamers. Then our mouths will be filled with laughter, and our tongues with glad song. Then will they declare among the nations: God has done great things for them. God has done great things for us: we were gladdened. O God, restore our exiles as springs in the Negev. Those who sow in tears will reap in glad song. He who bears a measure of seed goes along weeping, but he will return with exultation, bearing his sheaves.

Fear of Economic Insecurity Will Leave Us

The text of the Grace After Meals is not unique to Passover. As Jews, we thank God after every meal. Examining the words of this prayer, we will notice that the prevailing attitude expressed is one of confidence in God that He will provide for all of our needs.

We remember that our livelihood is solely in His hands. Financial security is not attained through human machinations or plotting. It is a gift bestowed from on high. And for that we are grateful. 🍷

BARECH

My mouth will utter the praise of God, and all flesh will bless His holy name forever and ever. And we will bless God from now and forever—Halleluyah! Give thanks to God for He is good, for His kindness is everlasting. Who can express the mighty acts of God? Who can declare all His praise?

תְּהִלַּת יְהֹוָה יְדַבֶּר־פִּי, וִיבָרֵךְ כָּל־בָּשָׂר שֵׁם קָדְשׁוֹ לְעוֹלָם וָעֶד: וַאֲנַחְנוּ נְבָרֵךְ יָהּ מֵעַתָּה וְעַד־עוֹלָם, הַלְלוּיָהּ: הוֹדוּ לַיהֹוָה כִּי טוֹב, כִּי לְעוֹלָם חַסְדּוֹ: מִי יְמַלֵּל גְּבוּרוֹת יְהֹוָה, יַשְׁמִיעַ כָּל־תְּהִלָּתוֹ:

(If there are fewer than three men skip to "Blessed are You.")
The leader says:

רַבּוֹתַי נְבָרֵךְ: — Gentlemen, let us say the blessings!

Everyone responds:

יְהִי שֵׁם יְהֹוָה מְבֹרָךְ מֵעַתָּה וְעַד־עוֹלָם: — May the name of God be blessed from now and forever.

The leader says (if ten men are present add the bracketed words):

בִּרְשׁוּת מָרָנָן וְרַבָּנָן וְרַבּוֹתַי נְבָרֵךְ [אֱלֹהֵינוּ] שֶׁאָכַלְנוּ מִשֶּׁלּוֹ: — With the permission of the masters, teachers, and gentlemen, let us bless He [our God] of Whose bounty we have eaten.

Everyone responds:

בָּרוּךְ [אֱלֹהֵינוּ] שֶׁאָכַלְנוּ מִשֶּׁלּוֹ וּבְטוּבוֹ חָיִינוּ: — Blessed be He [our God] of Whose bounty we have eaten and through Whose goodness we live.

The leader concludes:

בָּרוּךְ [אֱלֹהֵינוּ] שֶׁאָכַלְנוּ מִשֶּׁלּוֹ וּבְטוּבוֹ חָיִינוּ: — Blessed be He [our God] of Whose bounty we have eaten and through Whose goodness we live.

If ten men are present the leader says:

בָּרוּךְ הוּא וּבָרוּךְ שְׁמוֹ: — Blessed be He and blessed be His Name!

ברך

בָּרוּךְ אַתָּה יְהֹוָה אֱלֹהֵינוּ מֶלֶךְ הָעוֹלָם, הַזָּן אֶת־הָעוֹלָם כֻּלּוֹ בְּטוּבוֹ בְּחֵן בְּחֶסֶד וּבְרַחֲמִים, הוּא־נוֹתֵן לֶחֶם לְכָל־בָּשָׂר כִּי לְעוֹלָם חַסְדּוֹ: וּבְטוּבוֹ הַגָּדוֹל תָּמִיד לֹא חָסַר לָנוּ וְאַל יֶחְסַר־לָנוּ מָזוֹן לְעוֹלָם וָעֶד: בַּעֲבוּר שְׁמוֹ הַגָּדוֹל, כִּי הוּא אֵל זָן וּמְפַרְנֵס לַכֹּל וּמֵטִיב לַכֹּל וּמֵכִין מָזוֹן לְכָל־בְּרִיּוֹתָיו אֲשֶׁר בָּרָא: בָּרוּךְ אַתָּה יְהֹוָה, הַזָּן אֶת הַכֹּל:

נוֹדֶה לְךָ יְהֹוָה אֱלֹהֵינוּ עַל שֶׁהִנְחַלְתָּ לַאֲבוֹתֵינוּ אֶרֶץ חֶמְדָּה טוֹבָה וּרְחָבָה, וְעַל שֶׁהוֹצֵאתָנוּ יְהֹוָה אֱלֹהֵינוּ מֵאֶרֶץ מִצְרַיִם וּפְדִיתָנוּ מִבֵּית עֲבָדִים, וְעַל־בְּרִיתְךָ שֶׁחָתַמְתָּ בִּבְשָׂרֵנוּ וְעַל תּוֹרָתְךָ שֶׁלִּמַּדְתָּנוּ וְעַל חֻקֶּיךָ שֶׁהוֹדַעְתָּנוּ וְעַל חַיִּים חֵן וָחֶסֶד שֶׁחוֹנַנְתָּנוּ, וְעַל אֲכִילַת מָזוֹן שָׁאַתָּה זָן וּמְפַרְנֵס אוֹתָנוּ תָּמִיד בְּכָל־יוֹם וּבְכָל־עֵת וּבְכָל־שָׁעָה:

וְעַל הַכֹּל יְהֹוָה אֱלֹהֵינוּ אֲנַחְנוּ מוֹדִים לָךְ וּמְבָרְכִים אוֹתָךְ, יִתְבָּרַךְ שִׁמְךָ בְּפִי כָּל־חַי תָּמִיד לְעוֹלָם וָעֶד: כַּכָּתוּב, וְאָכַלְתָּ וְשָׂבָעְתָּ

Blessed are You, God, our God, King of the universe, Who feeds the whole world in His goodness, with grace, with kindness, and with mercy. He gives food to all flesh, for His kindness is everlasting. Through His great goodness, we have never lacked food, and may we never lack it for eternity. For the sake of His great name, because He is God Who feeds and sustains all, does good to all, and prepares food for all His creatures that He has created. Blessed are You, God, Who provides food for all.

We thank You, God, our God, for having given as a heritage to our ancestors a desirable, good, and spacious land; for having brought us out, God, our God, from the land of Egypt and redeemed us from the house of bondage; for Your covenant, which You have sealed in our flesh; for Your Torah, which You have taught us; for Your laws, which You have made known to us; for the life, grace, and kindness that You have bestowed upon us; and for the food we eat with which You constantly nourish and sustain us every day, in every season, and at every hour.

For all this, God, our God, we thank You and bless You. May Your Name be blessed by the mouth of every living being, constantly and for eternity—as the verse states: "You shall eat and

BARECH

וּבֵרַכְתָּ אֶת־יְהוָה אֱלֹהֶיךָ עַל־הָאָרֶץ הַטֹּבָה אֲשֶׁר נָתַן־לָךְ: בָּרוּךְ אַתָּה יְהוָה, עַל־הָאָרֶץ וְעַל־הַמָּזוֹן:

be satisfied, then you shall bless God, your God, for the good land that He has given you." Blessed are You, God, for the land and for the sustenance.

רַחֵם יְהוָה אֱלֹהֵינוּ עַל־יִשְׂרָאֵל עַמֶּךָ וְעַל־יְרוּשָׁלַיִם עִירֶךָ וְעַל־צִיּוֹן מִשְׁכַּן כְּבוֹדֶךָ וְעַל־מַלְכוּת בֵּית דָּוִד מְשִׁיחֶךָ, וְעַל־הַבַּיִת הַגָּדוֹל וְהַקָּדוֹשׁ שֶׁנִּקְרָא שִׁמְךָ עָלָיו: אֱלֹהֵינוּ אָבִינוּ רְעֵנוּ, זוּנֵנוּ פַּרְנְסֵנוּ וְכַלְכְּלֵנוּ וְהַרְוִיחֵנוּ וְהַרְוַח לָנוּ יְהוָה אֱלֹהֵינוּ מְהֵרָה מִכָּל־צָרוֹתֵינוּ: וְנָא אַל־תַּצְרִיכֵנוּ יְהוָה אֱלֹהֵינוּ לֹא לִידֵי מַתְּנַת בָּשָׂר וָדָם וְלֹא לִידֵי הַלְוָאָתָם, כִּי אִם לְיָדְךָ הַמְּלֵאָה הַפְּתוּחָה הַקְּדוֹשָׁה וְהָרְחָבָה, שֶׁלֹּא נֵבוֹשׁ וְלֹא נִכָּלֵם לְעוֹלָם וָעֶד:

Have mercy, God, our God, upon Israel, Your people; upon Jerusalem, Your city; upon Zion, the resting place of Your glory; upon the monarchy of the house of David, Your anointed; and upon the great and holy House that is called by Your name. Our God, our Father, our Shepherd! Sustain us, support us, nourish us, and relieve us! O God, our God, grant us speedy relief from all our misfortunes! O God, our God, please do not make us needful of the gifts of human hands nor of their loans, but of Your full, open, holy, and generous hand, so that we will not be shamed nor humiliated forever and ever.

On Shabbos add:

רְצֵה וְהַחֲלִיצֵנוּ יְהוָה אֱלֹהֵינוּ בְּמִצְוֹתֶיךָ וּבְמִצְוַת יוֹם הַשְּׁבִיעִי הַשַּׁבָּת הַגָּדוֹל וְהַקָּדוֹשׁ הַזֶּה. כִּי יוֹם זֶה גָּדוֹל וְקָדוֹשׁ הוּא לְפָנֶיךָ, לִשְׁבָּת־בּוֹ וְלָנוּחַ־בּוֹ בְּאַהֲבָה כְּמִצְוַת רְצוֹנֶךָ. וּבִרְצוֹנְךָ הָנִיחַ לָנוּ יְהוָה אֱלֹהֵינוּ שֶׁלֹּא תְהֵא צָרָה וְיָגוֹן וַאֲנָחָה בְּיוֹם מְנוּחָתֵנוּ. וְהַרְאֵנוּ יְהוָה אֱלֹהֵינוּ בְּנֶחָמַת צִיּוֹן עִירֶךָ, וּבְבִנְיַן יְרוּשָׁלַיִם

May it please You, God, our God, to fortify us through Your commandments, and through the commandment of the seventh day, this great and holy Shabbos. For this day is great and holy before You, to cease from work on it, and to rest on it, with love, according to the commandment of Your will. In Your will, God, our God, grant us tranquility, that there shall be no trouble, sorrow, or grief on the day of our rest. And let us see, God, our God, the consolation of Zion, Your city, and

עִיר קָדְשֶׁךָ, כִּי אַתָּה הוּא בַּעַל הַיְשׁוּעוֹת וּבַעַל הַנֶּחָמוֹת:

אֱלֹהֵינוּ וֵאלֹהֵי אֲבוֹתֵינוּ יַעֲלֶה וְיָבֹא, וְיַגִּיעַ וְיֵרָאֶה וְיֵרָצֶה, וְיִשָּׁמַע וְיִפָּקֵד וְיִזָּכֵר, זִכְרוֹנֵנוּ וּפִקְדוֹנֵנוּ, וְזִכְרוֹן אֲבוֹתֵינוּ, וְזִכְרוֹן מָשִׁיחַ בֶּן־דָּוִד עַבְדֶּךָ, וְזִכְרוֹן יְרוּשָׁלַיִם עִיר קָדְשֶׁךָ, וְזִכְרוֹן כָּל־עַמְּךָ בֵּית יִשְׂרָאֵל לְפָנֶיךָ, לִפְלֵיטָה לְטוֹבָה, לְחֵן וּלְחֶסֶד וּלְרַחֲמִים לְחַיִּים וּלְשָׁלוֹם, בְּיוֹם חַג הַמַּצּוֹת הַזֶּה. זָכְרֵנוּ יְהוָה אֱלֹהֵינוּ בּוֹ לְטוֹבָה, וּפָקְדֵנוּ בוֹ לִבְרָכָה, וְהוֹשִׁיעֵנוּ בוֹ לְחַיִּים: וּבִדְבַר יְשׁוּעָה וְרַחֲמִים חוּס וְחָנֵּנוּ וְרַחֵם עָלֵינוּ וְהוֹשִׁיעֵנוּ, כִּי אֵלֶיךָ עֵינֵינוּ, כִּי אֵל (מֶלֶךְ) חַנּוּן וְרַחוּם אָתָּה:

וּבְנֵה יְרוּשָׁלַיִם עִיר הַקֹּדֶשׁ בִּמְהֵרָה בְיָמֵינוּ. בָּרוּךְ אַתָּה יְהוָה בֹּנֶה בְרַחֲמָיו יְרוּשָׁלָיִם. אָמֵן:

בָּרוּךְ אַתָּה יְהוָה אֱלֹהֵינוּ מֶלֶךְ הָעוֹלָם, הָאֵל, אָבִינוּ מַלְכֵּנוּ, אַדִּירֵנוּ בּוֹרְאֵנוּ גּוֹאֲלֵנוּ יוֹצְרֵנוּ, קְדוֹשֵׁנוּ קְדוֹשׁ יַעֲקֹב רוֹעֵנוּ רוֹעֵה יִשְׂרָאֵל הַמֶּלֶךְ הַטּוֹב וְהַמֵּטִיב לַכֹּל שֶׁבְּכָל יוֹם וָיוֹם, הוּא הֵיטִיב, הוּא

the rebuilding of Jerusalem, Your holy city, for You are one Who works salvations and consolations.

Our God, and God of our ancestors, may the remembrance and recollection of us, the remembrance of our ancestors, the remembrance of Mashiach the descendant of David, Your servant, the remembrance of Jerusalem, Your holy city, and the remembrance of all Your people, the House of Israel, rise, come, reach, be noted, favored, heard, recalled, and remembered before You, for deliverance, well-being, grace, lovingkindness, mercy, life, and peace, on this day of the Festival of Matzos. Remember us on it, God, our God, for good; call us to mind on it for blessing; save us on it for life. With the promise of deliverance and compassion, save us and be gracious to us; have mercy upon us and save us. For our eyes are turned to You, for You, God, are a gracious and merciful King.

Rebuild Jerusalem, the holy city, speedily in our days. Blessed are You, God, Who in His mercy rebuilds Jerusalem. Amen.

Blessed are You, God, our God, King of the universe: God, our Father, our King; our Sovereign, our Creator, our Redeemer, our Maker; our Holy One, the Holy One of Jacob, our Shepherd, the Shepherd of Israel, the King Who is good and does good to all, each day. He has done good, He does good, and

BARECH

He will do good for us. He has bestowed, He bestows, and He will forever bestow upon us with grace, kindness, and mercy; relief, salvation, and success; blessing and salvation; consolation, sustenance, and nourishment; compassion, life, peace, and all goodness; and may He never let us lack any good.

מֵטִיב, הוּא יֵיטִיב לָנוּ, הוּא גְמָלָנוּ הוּא גוֹמְלֵנוּ הוּא יִגְמְלֵנוּ לָעַד, לְחֵן וּלְחֶסֶד וּלְרַחֲמִים, וּלְרֶוַח הַצָּלָה וְהַצְלָחָה, בְּרָכָה וִישׁוּעָה, נֶחָמָה פַּרְנָסָה וְכַלְכָּלָה וְרַחֲמִים וְחַיִּים וְשָׁלוֹם וְכָל־טוֹב, וּמִכָּל־טוּב לְעוֹלָם אַל יְחַסְּרֵנוּ:

May the Merciful One reign over us forever and ever. May the Merciful One be blessed in heaven and on earth. May the Merciful One be praised for generations, and be glorified through us eternally, and honored through us forever. May the Merciful One sustain us in honor. May the Merciful One break the oppressive yoke from our neck and may He lead us upright to our land. May the Merciful One send us abundant blessing into this house and upon this table at which we have eaten. May the Merciful One send us the Prophet Elijah, may he be remembered for good, who will bring us good tidings, salvation, and comfort.

הָרַחֲמָן הוּא יִמְלֹךְ עָלֵינוּ לְעוֹלָם וָעֶד: הָרַחֲמָן הוּא יִתְבָּרַךְ בַּשָּׁמַיִם וּבָאָרֶץ: הָרַחֲמָן הוּא יִשְׁתַּבַּח לְדוֹר דּוֹרִים וְיִתְפָּאַר בָּנוּ לָעַד וּלְנֵצַח נְצָחִים וְיִתְהַדַּר בָּנוּ לָעַד וּלְעוֹלְמֵי עוֹלָמִים: הָרַחֲמָן הוּא יְפַרְנְסֵנוּ בְּכָבוֹד: הָרַחֲמָן הוּא יִשְׁבּוֹר עֻלֵּנוּ מֵעַל צַוָּארֵנוּ וְהוּא יוֹלִיכֵנוּ קוֹמְמִיּוּת לְאַרְצֵנוּ: הָרַחֲמָן הוּא יִשְׁלַח לָנוּ בְּרָכָה מְרֻבָּה בַּבַּיִת הַזֶּה וְעַל שֻׁלְחָן זֶה שֶׁאָכַלְנוּ עָלָיו: הָרַחֲמָן הוּא יִשְׁלַח לָנוּ אֶת־אֵלִיָּהוּ הַנָּבִיא זָכוּר לַטּוֹב, וִיבַשֶּׂר־לָנוּ בְּשׂוֹרוֹת טוֹבוֹת יְשׁוּעוֹת וְנֶחָמוֹת:

Those eating at home say the following (including words that apply).

May the Merciful One bless me (and my father and mother) (and my wife/husband and my children) and all that belongs to me.

הָרַחֲמָן הוּא יְבָרֵךְ אוֹתִי (וְאָבִי וְאִמִּי) (וְאֶת־אִשְׁתִּי / בַּעֲלִי וְאֶת־זַרְעִי) וְאֶת־כָּל־אֲשֶׁר לִי.

Guests recite the following (children at their parents' table add the words in parentheses).

הָרַחֲמָן, הוּא יְבָרֵךְ אֶת (אָבִי מוֹרִי) בַּעַל הַבַּיִת הַזֶּה, וְאֶת (אִמִּי מוֹרָתִי) אִשְׁתּוֹ בַּעֲלַת הַבַּיִת הַזֶּה, אוֹתָם וְאֶת־בֵּיתָם וְאֶת־זַרְעָם וְאֶת־כָּל־אֲשֶׁר לָהֶם,

May the Merciful One bless (my father, my teacher) the master of this house, and (my mother, my teacher) the lady of this house; them and their household, their children, and all that belongs to them.

All continue:

אוֹתָנוּ וְאֶת־כָּל־אֲשֶׁר לָנוּ: כְּמוֹ שֶׁנִּתְבָּרְכוּ אֶת־אֲבוֹתֵינוּ אַבְרָהָם יִצְחָק וְיַעֲקֹב בַּכֹּל מִכֹּל כֹּל, כֵּן יְבָרֵךְ אוֹתָנוּ כֻּלָּנוּ יַחַד בִּבְרָכָה שְׁלֵמָה, וְנֹאמַר אָמֵן:

Ours, and all that is ours, just as our forefathers, Abraham, Isaac, and Jacob, were blessed in everything, through everything, and with everything, so may He bless all of us together with a perfect blessing. And let us say, Amen.

בַּמָּרוֹם יְלַמְּדוּ עֲלֵיהֶם וְעָלֵינוּ זְכוּת שֶׁתְּהֵא לְמִשְׁמֶרֶת שָׁלוֹם, וְנִשָּׂא בְרָכָה מֵאֵת יְהֹוָה וּצְדָקָה מֵאֱלֹהֵי יִשְׁעֵנוּ, וְנִמְצָא חֵן וְשֵׂכֶל טוֹב בְּעֵינֵי אֱלֹהִים וְאָדָם:

On high, may there be pleaded for them and for us such merit so as to make a sure guarantee of peace. May we obtain a blessing from God, and just kindness from the God of our salvation, and may we find grace and good understanding in the eyes of God and man.

On Shabbos add:

הָרַחֲמָן הוּא יַנְחִילֵנוּ יוֹם שֶׁכֻּלוֹ שַׁבָּת וּמְנוּחָה לְחַיֵּי הָעוֹלָמִים:

May the Merciful One bring us to inherit the day that will be entirely Shabbos and rest for eternal life.

הָרַחֲמָן הוּא יַנְחִילֵנוּ יוֹם שֶׁכֻּלוֹ טוֹב (יוֹם שֶׁכֻּלוֹ אָרוּךְ, יוֹם שֶׁצַּדִּיקִים יוֹשְׁבִים וְעַטְרוֹתֵיהֶם בְּרָאשֵׁיהֶם וְנֶהֱנִים מִזִּיו הַשְּׁכִינָה, וִיהִי חֶלְקֵנוּ עִמָּהֶם):

May the Merciful One bring us to inherit that day that is entirely good (that everlasting day, the day when the righteous sit with crowns on their heads, enjoying the radiance of the Divine Presence, and may our portion be with them)!

BARECH

May the Merciful One merit us with the days of Mashiach and life in the World to Come. "He is a tower of salvation for His king, and bestows kindness on His anointed, to David and his seed forever." He Who makes peace in His heights, may He grant peace for us and for all Israel. And let us say, Amen.

הָרַחֲמָן הוּא יְזַכֵּנוּ לִימוֹת הַמָּשִׁיחַ וּלְחַיֵּי הָעוֹלָם הַבָּא. מִגְדֹּל יְשׁוּעוֹת מַלְכּוֹ וְעֹשֶׂה־חֶסֶד לִמְשִׁיחוֹ לְדָוִד וּלְזַרְעוֹ עַד־עוֹלָם: עֹשֶׂה שָׁלוֹם בִּמְרוֹמָיו הוּא יַעֲשֶׂה שָׁלוֹם עָלֵינוּ וְעַל כָּל־יִשְׂרָאֵל וְאִמְרוּ אָמֵן:

Fear God, you His holy ones, for those who fear Him lack nothing. Young lions are in need and go hungry, but those who seek God shall not lack any good. Give thanks to God for He is good, for His kindness is everlasting. You open Your hand and satisfy the desire of every living thing. Blessed is the man who trusts in God, and God will become his trust. I was a youth and also have aged, and I have not seen a righteous man forsaken, with his children begging for bread. God will give might to His nation. God will bless His nation with peace.

יְראוּ אֶת־יְהֹוָה קְדֹשָׁיו, כִּי־אֵין מַחְסוֹר לִירֵאָיו: כְּפִירִים רָשׁוּ וְרָעֵבוּ, וְדֹרְשֵׁי יְהֹוָה לֹא־יַחְסְרוּ כָל־טוֹב: הוֹדוּ לַיהֹוָה כִּי־טוֹב, כִּי לְעוֹלָם חַסְדּוֹ: פּוֹתֵחַ אֶת־יָדֶךָ, וּמַשְׂבִּיעַ לְכָל־חַי רָצוֹן: בָּרוּךְ הַגֶּבֶר אֲשֶׁר יִבְטַח בַּיהֹוָה, וְהָיָה יְהֹוָה מִבְטַחוֹ: נַעַר הָיִיתִי גַּם־זָקַנְתִּי, וְלֹא־רָאִיתִי צַדִּיק נֶעֱזָב, וְזַרְעוֹ מְבַקֶּשׁ־לָחֶם: יְהֹוָה עֹז לְעַמּוֹ יִתֵּן, יְהֹוָה יְבָרֵךְ אֶת־עַמּוֹ בַשָּׁלוֹם:

Hold the cup in your right hand.

Blessed are You, God, our God, King of the universe, Who creates the fruit of the vine.

בָּרוּךְ אַתָּה יְהֹוָה אֱלֹהֵינוּ מֶלֶךְ הָעוֹלָם, בּוֹרֵא פְּרִי הַגָּפֶן:

- Recline to the left and drink the cup (as before).
- The cup of Elijah is poured. The fourth cup of wine is poured.

בָּרֵךְ

שְׁפֹךְ חֲמָתְךָ / Pour out Your anger

אֶל־הַגּוֹיִם אֲשֶׁר לֹא־יְדָעוּךָ, וְעַל מַמְלָכוֹת אֲשֶׁר בְּשִׁמְךָ לֹא קָרָאוּ: כִּי אָכַל אֶת־יַעֲקֹב, וְאֶת־נָוֵהוּ הֵשַׁמּוּ:

upon the nations that do not recognize You, and upon the kingdoms that do not call upon Your Name. For they have devoured Jacob and laid waste his dwelling place.[74]

A Vision for the World

At this point in the Seder, we open the door for Elijah the Prophet, who visits every home where a Seder is held. There are many reasons for this custom. However, the primary meaning is as follows:

Elijah, our tradition explains, will be the one to announce Mashiach's imminent arrival.[75] Therefore, opening the door for him is an expression of our faith in the complete redemption of all humanity, which will come about through Mashiach.[76]

We are grateful to be gathered together to celebrate our freedom. However, we remember that there are those who still suffer and will continue to suffer until such time that the world is finally perfected.

One of our most basic beliefs as Jews is that there will come a time when all people will be free—a time of universal enlightenment and God consciousness. As much as we savor our own personal freedom, we know that it is not complete and will not ever be complete until every single person is free.

BARECH

שְׁפֹךְ־עֲלֵיהֶם זַעְמֶךָ, וַחֲרוֹן אַפְּךָ יַשִּׂיגֵם: תִּרְדֹּף בְּאַף וְתַשְׁמִידֵם מִתַּחַת שְׁמֵי יְהוָה:

Pour out Your indignation upon them, and let Your fierce anger overtake them.[77] Pursue them with wrath, and destroy them from beneath the heavens of God.[78]

A Worthy Prayer

There is a tradition that tells us that when the door is open for Elijah, the doors of prayer are open as well, and one may ask for anything at all.

One of the great Chasidic masters once told his son: "Yosef Yitzchak [during the Seder], in particular when the doors are opened, we must think about being a Mentsh, and God will help. Don't ask for material things; ask for spiritual things."[79]

In recovery, we have become accustomed to turn to God often in prayer. Our Tenth Step enjoins us to improve our conscious contact with God through prayer and meditation. But we have learned that the most important things to pray for are not material. We pray for spiritual help and strength. As the Tenth Step says, "praying only for knowledge of God's will for us and the power to carry that out."

When we will fulfill God's will, all material blessings will automatically appear in our lives.

Revealing Elijah

A Jew once went to the holy Baal Shem Tov and said, "Rebbe, I want to experience the revelation of Elijah the Prophet."

The Baal Shem Tov replied, "Fill a box with food and another box with children's clothing. Then, before Rosh Hashanah, travel to the city of Minsk. On the outskirts of town at the edge of the forest, you will find an old, dilapidated shack. Don't knock on the door immediately. Rather, stand there and listen. Then, shortly before candle lighting, knock on the door and ask whoever answers to let you in and host you."

The Jew went home and told his wife what the Baal Shem Tov had told him. When she asked how he could give up spending Rosh Hashanah with his family, he replied, "How can I give up a once-in-a-lifetime opportunity to see a revelation of Elijah the Prophet?"

After discussing it further, his wife finally agreed that he could not pass up this opportunity. He carried out the Baal Shem Tov's instructions and traveled to Minsk.

He found the house and, as instructed, he waited outside for some time before knocking on the door.

He heard voices from within. A child was crying, "Mommy, we're hungry. The festival is coming, and we don't even have food to eat. We also don't have nice clothing to wear."

He then heard a mother's voice reply, "Children, trust in God; He will surely take care of us."

The Jew then knocked on the door. When the woman opened it, he asked if he could be their guest for the festival. "How can we host you when we don't have any food?" she asked.

"Don't worry," he said. "I've brought enough food for all of us, and I even have new clothing for your children."

The children opened the boxes and tried on the clothing with delight, and they ate the food that the man had brought.

As for him, he waited with bated breath for the moment when he would catch a glimpse of Elijah the Prophet as a reward for following the Baal Shem Tov's instructions. However, Rosh

Hashanah came and went without his seeing any revelations. Disappointed, he returned to the Baal Shem Tov and lamented, "Rebbe, I did exactly as instructed, but I did not see Elijah the Prophet."

"Did you do exactly as I instructed?" asked the Baal Shem Tov.

"Yes."

"And you're sure you didn't see Elijah the Prophet?"

"I'm quite certain," the man replied.

"In that case," said the Baal Shem Tov, "go back before Yom Kippur and bring along another box of food and a box of clothing. Make sure to arrive an hour before sunset, and don't knock immediately. Just wait outside for some time before you make your presence known."

The Jew went back to his wife and told her he would be away for Yom Kippur as well. He simply could not pass up the opportunity to see Elijah the Prophet.

His wife agreed that it was an opportunity too great to pass up.

He went back to Minsk, and on the day before Yom Kippur he returned to the house and stood outside. He heard voices from inside. One of the children said, "Mommy, we're hungry. We haven't eaten all day. How can we fast on Yom Kippur?"

"Children," the mother replied, "don't you remember how, just days ago, right before Rosh Hashanah, you cried that you had no food or clothing and I told you to trust in God? Well, I am telling you the same thing now. Just as God sent us Elijah the Prophet before Rosh Hashanah, He will certainly send Elijah again today!"

At that moment, the man understood very well what it meant to behold the revelation of Elijah the Prophet. And this is a lesson for us as well. Sometimes the greatest way to *see* Elijah the Prophet is to *be* Elijah the Prophet. As we have come to learn, when it comes to experiencing new spiritual heights there is no path as tried and true as service to others.

SEDER STEP 14
HALLEL

PRAISE

לֹא לָנוּ

יְהוָה לֹא־לָנוּ, כִּי לְשִׁמְךָ תֵּן כָּבוֹד, עַל־חַסְדְּךָ עַל־אֲמִתֶּךָ: לָמָּה יֹאמְרוּ הַגּוֹיִם, אַיֵּה־נָא אֱלֹהֵיהֶם: וֵאלֹהֵינוּ בַשָּׁמָיִם, כֹּל אֲשֶׁר־חָפֵץ עָשָׂה: עֲצַבֵּיהֶם כֶּסֶף וְזָהָב, מַעֲשֵׂה יְדֵי אָדָם: פֶּה־לָהֶם וְלֹא יְדַבֵּרוּ, עֵינַיִם לָהֶם וְלֹא יִרְאוּ: אָזְנַיִם לָהֶם וְלֹא יִשְׁמָעוּ, אַף לָהֶם וְלֹא יְרִיחוּן: יְדֵיהֶם וְלֹא יְמִישׁוּן, רַגְלֵיהֶם וְלֹא יְהַלֵּכוּ, לֹא־יֶהְגּוּ בִּגְרוֹנָם: כְּמוֹהֶם יִהְיוּ עֹשֵׂיהֶם, כֹּל אֲשֶׁר־בֹּטֵחַ בָּהֶם: יִשְׂרָאֵל בְּטַח בַּיהוָה, עֶזְרָם וּמָגִנָּם

Not for

our sake, God, not for our sake, but for Your Name's sake give glory, for the sake of Your kindness and Your truth. Why should the nations say, "Where is their God?" Our God is in heaven; He has done whatever He has desired. Their idols are silver and gold, the work of human hands. They have mouths, but they do not speak; they have eyes, but they do not see; they have ears, but they do not hear; they have a nose, but they do not smell; hands, but they do not feel; feet, but they do not walk; they make no sound with their throat. Those who make them will become like them, whoever trusts in them. Israel, trust in God! He is their

Giving Praise

"Hallel" means "praise." We conclude our Seder by praising God. Yes, this is our story, the story of our liberation, but we did not free ourselves. We humbly remember that it was God and God alone Who redeemed us and Who is worthy of all praise. ♦

HALLEL

help and their shield. House of Aaron, trust in God! He is their help and their shield. Those who fear God, trust in God! He is their help and their shield.

God, Who has remembered us, will bless. He will bless the House of Israel; He will bless the House of Aaron; He will bless those who fear God, the small with the great. May God add upon you—upon you and upon your children. You are blessed by God, the Maker of heaven and earth. The heavens are the heavens of God, but the earth He has given to mankind. The dead cannot praise God, nor can those who descend into silence. But we will bless God, from now and forever. Halleluyah!

I love God, because He hears my voice and my prayers. For He has inclined His ear to me, so all my days I will call upon Him. The cords of death surrounded me, and the pains of the grave came upon me. Trouble and sorrow I encountered. Then I called the name of God: Please, God, deliver my soul! God is gracious and just, and our God is compassionate. God protects the simple. I was brought low and He saved me. Return to your rest, O my soul, for God has dealt kindly with you. For You have delivered my soul from death, my eyes from tears, my feet from stumbling. I will walk before

הוּא: בֵּית אַהֲרֹן בִּטְחוּ בַיהוָה, עֶזְרָם וּמָגִנָּם הוּא: יִרְאֵי יְהוָה בִּטְחוּ בַיהוָה, עֶזְרָם וּמָגִנָּם הוּא:

יְהוָה זְכָרָנוּ יְבָרֵךְ, יְבָרֵךְ אֶת־בֵּית יִשְׂרָאֵל, יְבָרֵךְ אֶת־בֵּית אַהֲרֹן: יְבָרֵךְ יִרְאֵי יְהוָה, הַקְּטַנִּים עִם־הַגְּדֹלִים: יֹסֵף יְהוָה עֲלֵיכֶם, עֲלֵיכֶם וְעַל־בְּנֵיכֶם: בְּרוּכִים אַתֶּם לַיהוָה, עֹשֵׂה שָׁמַיִם וָאָרֶץ: הַשָּׁמַיִם שָׁמַיִם לַיהוָה, וְהָאָרֶץ נָתַן לִבְנֵי־אָדָם: לֹא הַמֵּתִים יְהַלְלוּ־יָהּ, וְלֹא כָּל־יֹרְדֵי דוּמָה: וַאֲנַחְנוּ נְבָרֵךְ יָהּ מֵעַתָּה וְעַד־עוֹלָם, הַלְלוּיָהּ:

אָהַבְתִּי כִּי־יִשְׁמַע יְהוָה אֶת־קוֹלִי תַּחֲנוּנָי: כִּי־הִטָּה אָזְנוֹ לִי, וּבְיָמַי אֶקְרָא: אֲפָפוּנִי חֶבְלֵי־מָוֶת וּמְצָרֵי שְׁאוֹל מְצָאוּנִי, צָרָה וְיָגוֹן אֶמְצָא: וּבְשֵׁם־יְהוָה אֶקְרָא, אָנָּה יְהוָה מַלְּטָה נַפְשִׁי: חַנּוּן יְהוָה וְצַדִּיק, וֵאלֹהֵינוּ מְרַחֵם: שֹׁמֵר פְּתָאיִם יְהוָה, דַּלּוֹתִי וְלִי יְהוֹשִׁיעַ: שׁוּבִי נַפְשִׁי לִמְנוּחָיְכִי, כִּי־יְהוָה גָּמַל עָלָיְכִי: כִּי חִלַּצְתָּ נַפְשִׁי מִמָּוֶת, אֶת־עֵינִי מִן־דִּמְעָה, אֶת־רַגְלִי מִדֶּחִי: אֶתְהַלֵּךְ לִפְנֵי

יְהֹוָה, בְּאַרְצוֹת הַחַיִּים: הֶאֱמַנְתִּי כִּי אֲדַבֵּר, אֲנִי עָנִיתִי מְאֹד: אֲנִי אָמַרְתִּי בְחָפְזִי, כָּל־הָאָדָם כֹּזֵב:

מָה־אָשִׁיב לַיהֹוָה, כָּל־תַּגְמוּלוֹהִי עָלָי: כּוֹס־יְשׁוּעוֹת אֶשָּׂא, וּבְשֵׁם יְהֹוָה אֶקְרָא: נְדָרַי לַיהֹוָה אֲשַׁלֵּם, נֶגְדָה־נָּא לְכָל־עַמּוֹ: יָקָר בְּעֵינֵי יְהֹוָה, הַמָּוְתָה לַחֲסִידָיו: אָנָּה יְהֹוָה כִּי־אֲנִי עַבְדֶּךָ, אֲנִי עַבְדְּךָ בֶּן־אֲמָתֶךָ, פִּתַּחְתָּ לְמוֹסֵרָי: לְךָ אֶזְבַּח זֶבַח תּוֹדָה, וּבְשֵׁם יְהֹוָה אֶקְרָא: נְדָרַי לַיהֹוָה אֲשַׁלֵּם, נֶגְדָה־נָּא לְכָל־עַמּוֹ: בְּחַצְרוֹת בֵּית יְהֹוָה בְּתוֹכֵכִי יְרוּשָׁלָיִם, הַלְלוּיָהּ:

הַלְלוּ אֶת־יְהֹוָה כָּל־גּוֹיִם, שַׁבְּחוּהוּ כָּל־הָאֻמִּים: כִּי גָבַר עָלֵינוּ חַסְדּוֹ, וֶאֱמֶת־יְהֹוָה לְעוֹלָם, הַלְלוּיָהּ:

God in the land of the living. I kept faith even when I said, "I am greatly afflicted." It was in my haste that I said, "All men are false."

What could I repay God for all His kindness to me? I will raise the cup of salvation and call upon the name of God. I will pay my vows to God now in the presence of all His people. Precious in the eyes of God is the death of His pious ones. I thank you, God, for I am Your servant. I am Your servant the child of Your handmaiden; You have loosened my bonds. To You I will bring a thanksgiving sacrifice, and I will call upon the Name of God. I will pay my vows to God in the presence of all His people, in the courtyards of the House of God, in the midst of Jerusalem. Halleluyah!

Praise God, all you nations! Praise Him, all you peoples! For His kindness to us was great, and the truth of God endures forever. Halleluyah!

- After each of the following four lines is chanted by the leader, all others respond out loud: "Give thanks to God for He is good, for His kindness is everlasting."

הוֹדוּ לַיהֹוָה כִּי טוֹב, כִּי לְעוֹלָם חַסְדּוֹ:

יֹאמַר־נָא יִשְׂרָאֵל, כִּי לְעוֹלָם חַסְדּוֹ:

Give thanks to God for He is good, for His kindness is everlasting.

Let Israel say, "For His kindness is everlasting."

HALLEL

יֹאמְרוּ נָא בֵית־אַהֲרֹן, כִּי לְעוֹלָם חַסְדּוֹ:

יֹאמְרוּ נָא יִרְאֵי יְהֹוָה, כִּי לְעוֹלָם חַסְדּוֹ:

מִן־הַמֵּצַר קָרָאתִי יָּהּ, עָנָנִי בַמֶּרְחָב יָהּ: יְהֹוָה לִי לֹא אִירָא, מַה־יַּעֲשֶׂה לִי אָדָם: יְהֹוָה לִי בְּעֹזְרָי, וַאֲנִי אֶרְאֶה בְשֹׂנְאָי: טוֹב לַחֲסוֹת בַּיהֹוָה מִבְּטֹחַ בָּאָדָם: טוֹב לַחֲסוֹת בַּיהֹוָה מִבְּטֹחַ בִּנְדִיבִים: כָּל־גּוֹיִם סְבָבוּנִי, בְּשֵׁם יְהֹוָה כִּי אֲמִילַם: סַבּוּנִי גַם־סְבָבוּנִי, בְּשֵׁם יְהֹוָה כִּי אֲמִילַם: סַבּוּנִי כִדְבֹרִים דֹּעֲכוּ כְּאֵשׁ קוֹצִים, בְּשֵׁם יְהֹוָה כִּי אֲמִילַם: דָּחֹה דְחִיתַנִי לִנְפֹּל, וַיהֹוָה עֲזָרָנִי: עָזִּי וְזִמְרָת יָהּ, וַיְהִי־לִי לִישׁוּעָה: קוֹל רִנָּה וִישׁוּעָה בְּאָהֳלֵי צַדִּיקִים, יְמִין יְהֹוָה עֹשָׂה חָיִל: יְמִין יְהֹוָה רוֹמֵמָה, יְמִין יְהֹוָה עֹשָׂה חָיִל: לֹא־אָמוּת כִּי־אֶחְיֶה, וַאֲסַפֵּר מַעֲשֵׂי יָהּ: יַסֹּר יִסְּרַנִּי יָּהּ, וְלַמָּוֶת לֹא נְתָנָנִי: פִּתְחוּ־לִי שַׁעֲרֵי־צֶדֶק, אָבֹא־בָם אוֹדֶה יָהּ: זֶה־הַשַּׁעַר לַיהֹוָה, צַדִּיקִים יָבֹאוּ בוֹ:

Let the House of Aaron say, "For His kindness is everlasting."

Let those who fear God say, "For His kindness is everlasting."

Out of the straits I called upon God; God answered me with expansiveness. God is with me, I will not fear. What can man do to me? God is for me, through my helpers. Therefore, I can look upon those who hate me. It is better to rely on God than to trust in man. It is better to rely on God than to trust in princes. All nations surrounded me, but in the name of God I cut them down. They surrounded me, they also encompassed me, but in the name of God I cut them down. They surrounded me like bees, but they were quenched like a fire of thorns, for in the name of God I cut them down. You pushed me again and again to make me fall, but God helped me. God is my strength and song; He has been my salvation. The voice of joy and salvation is in the tents of the righteous, "God's right hand does valiantly! God's right hand is exalted! God's right hand makes war!" I shall not die but live and tell the works of God. God has chastised me, but He did not give me over to death. Open for me the gates of righteousness. I will go into them and give thanks to God. This is the gate of God; the righteous will enter it.

אוֹדְךָ כִּי עֲנִיתָנִי,
וַתְּהִי־לִי לִישׁוּעָה
(repeat):
אֶבֶן מָאֲסוּ הַבּוֹנִים,
הָיְתָה לְרֹאשׁ פִּנָּה
(repeat):
מֵאֵת יְהוָה הָיְתָה זֹּאת,
הִיא נִפְלָאת בְּעֵינֵינוּ
(repeat):
זֶה־הַיּוֹם עָשָׂה יְהוָה,
נָגִילָה וְנִשְׂמְחָה בוֹ
(repeat):

I thank You for You have answered me, and You have become my salvation (repeat).
The stone that the builders rejected has become the main cornerstone (repeat).
This was indeed from God, it is marvelous in our eyes (repeat).
This is the day that God has made, let us be glad and rejoice on it (repeat).

The following is said responsively.

אָנָּא יְהוָה הוֹשִׁיעָה נָּא:	Please save us, God!
אָנָּא יְהוָה הוֹשִׁיעָה נָּא:	Please save us, God!
אָנָּא יְהוָה הַצְלִיחָה נָּא:	Please grant us success, God!
אָנָּא יְהוָה הַצְלִיחָה נָּא:	Please grant us success, God!

Gifts in Disguise

No one would purposely choose to hit rock bottom in order to have a spiritual awakening. However, in retrospect, we now look back and are grateful for everything that has happened to us. As the Ninth Step tells us, "No matter how far down the scale we have gone, we will see how our experience can benefit others. We will not regret the past nor choose to shut the door on it."

The degradation and humiliation of the past were experiences that we may have wanted to reject when they happened to us. However, we see now that they are the cornerstones upon which we build our new life.

HALLEL

בָּרוּךְ הַבָּא בְּשֵׁם יְהֹוָה, בֵּרַכְנוּכֶם מִבֵּית יְהֹוָה (repeat):
אֵל יְהֹוָה וַיָּאֶר לָנוּ, אִסְרוּ־חַג בַּעֲבֹתִים עַד־קַרְנוֹת הַמִּזְבֵּחַ (repeat):
אֵלִי אַתָּה וְאוֹדֶךָּ, אֱלֹהַי אֲרוֹמְמֶךָּ (repeat):
הוֹדוּ לַיהֹוָה כִּי־טוֹב, כִּי לְעוֹלָם חַסְדּוֹ (repeat):

יְהַלְלוּךָ יְהֹוָה אֱלֹהֵינוּ (עַל) כָּל־מַעֲשֶׂיךָ וַחֲסִידֶיךָ צַדִּיקִים עוֹשֵׂי רְצוֹנֶךָ, וְכָל־עַמְּךָ בֵּית יִשְׂרָאֵל בְּרִנָּה יוֹדוּ וִיבָרְכוּ וִישַׁבְּחוּ וִיפָאֲרוּ וִירוֹמְמוּ וְיַעֲרִיצוּ וְיַקְדִּישׁוּ וְיַמְלִיכוּ אֶת־שִׁמְךָ מַלְכֵּנוּ. כִּי לְךָ טוֹב לְהוֹדוֹת וּלְשִׁמְךָ נָאֶה לְזַמֵּר כִּי מֵעוֹלָם וְעַד עוֹלָם אַתָּה אֵל:

הוֹדוּ לַיהֹוָה כִּי־טוֹב, כִּי לְעוֹלָם חַסְדּוֹ:

הוֹדוּ לֵאלֹהֵי הָאֱלֹהִים, כִּי לְעוֹלָם חַסְדּוֹ:

Blessed is he who comes in the name of God; we bless you out of the House of God (repeat).
God is God, Who has shown us light; bind the festival sacrifice with cords to the horns of the altar (repeat).
You are my God and I will thank You; my God, I will exalt You (repeat).
Give thanks to God for He is good, for His kindness is everlasting (repeat).

May all your works praise You, God, our God, with your pious ones, the righteous, who do Your will. May all Your people, the House of Israel, give joyful thanks, bless, praise, glorify, exalt, adore, sanctify, and proclaim the sovereignty of Your Name, our King. For it is good to give You thanks, and befitting to sing to Your Name, because forever and for eternity You are God.

Give thanks to God for He is good
—for His kindness is everlasting;

Give thanks to the God of gods
—for His kindness is everlasting;

The Wonders We Don't Know

There is a deeper meaning of the verse "Who alone does great wonders": Not only is God the only one Who makes wonders, but sometimes He is the only one Who even knows about the wonders He has made.[80]

We reflect upon the miracles that God has done for us—both the ones we know about and the ones we do not know

הוֹדוּ לַאדֹנֵי הָאֲדֹנִים, כִּי לְעוֹלָם חַסְדּוֹ:	Give thanks to the Master of masters —for His kindness is everlasting:
לְעֹשֵׂה נִפְלָאוֹת גְּדֹלוֹת לְבַדּוֹ, כִּי לְעוֹלָם חַסְדּוֹ:	Who alone does great wonders —for His kindness is everlasting;
לְעֹשֵׂה הַשָּׁמַיִם בִּתְבוּנָה, כִּי לְעוֹלָם חַסְדּוֹ:	Who made the heavens with understanding —for His kindness is everlasting;
לְרוֹקַע הָאָרֶץ עַל־הַמָּיִם, כִּי לְעוֹלָם חַסְדּוֹ:	Who stretched out the earth over the waters —for His kindness is everlasting;
לְעֹשֵׂה אוֹרִים גְּדֹלִים, כִּי לְעוֹלָם חַסְדּוֹ:	Who made the great lights —for His kindness is everlasting;
אֶת־הַשֶּׁמֶשׁ לְמֶמְשֶׁלֶת בַּיּוֹם, כִּי לְעוֹלָם חַסְדּוֹ:	The sun, to rule by day —for His kindness is everlasting;
אֶת־הַיָּרֵחַ וְכוֹכָבִים לְמֶמְשְׁלוֹת בַּלָּיְלָה, כִּי לְעוֹלָם חַסְדּוֹ:	The moon and stars, to rule by night —for His kindness is everlasting;
לְמַכֵּה מִצְרַיִם בִּבְכוֹרֵיהֶם, כִּי לְעוֹלָם חַסְדּוֹ:	Who struck Egypt through their firstborn —for His kindness is everlasting;
וַיּוֹצֵא יִשְׂרָאֵל מִתּוֹכָם, כִּי לְעוֹלָם חַסְדּוֹ:	And brought Israel out from among them —for His kindness is everlasting;
בְּיָד חֲזָקָה וּבִזְרוֹעַ נְטוּיָה, כִּי לְעוֹלָם חַסְדּוֹ:	With a strong hand and an outstretched arm —for His kindness is everlasting;

about. It should not surprise us that since God is infinite, He is beyond the grasp of our intellect. That which we can appreciate is but a glimmer of His true kindness. There is infinitely more that He is doing for us that is completely beyond our ability to comprehend.

Yet, our inability to understand these wonders does not prevent us from having gratitude for these types of wonders as well. We therefore express our thanks for all the wonders—those that are known to us and those that are only known to God. ♦

HALLEL

לְגֹזֵר יַם־סוּף לִגְזָרִים,
כִּי לְעוֹלָם חַסְדּוֹ:

Who split the Sea of Reeds into parts
—for His kindness is everlasting;

וְהֶעֱבִיר יִשְׂרָאֵל בְּתוֹכוֹ,
כִּי לְעוֹלָם חַסְדּוֹ:

And led Israel right through it
—for His kindness is everlasting;

וְנִעֵר פַּרְעֹה וְחֵילוֹ בְיַם־סוּף,
כִּי לְעוֹלָם חַסְדּוֹ:

And cast Pharaoh and his army into the Sea of Reeds
—for His kindness is everlasting;

לְמוֹלִיךְ עַמּוֹ בַּמִּדְבָּר,
כִּי לְעוֹלָם חַסְדּוֹ:

Who led His people through the desert
—for His kindness is everlasting;

לְמַכֵּה מְלָכִים גְּדֹלִים,
כִּי לְעוֹלָם חַסְדּוֹ:

Who struck great kings
—for His kindness is everlasting;

וַיַּהֲרֹג מְלָכִים אַדִּירִים,
כִּי לְעוֹלָם חַסְדּוֹ:

And slew mighty kings
—for His kindness is everlasting;

לְסִיחוֹן מֶלֶךְ הָאֱמֹרִי,
כִּי לְעוֹלָם חַסְדּוֹ:

Sichon, king of the Emori
—for His kindness is everlasting;

וּלְעוֹג מֶלֶךְ הַבָּשָׁן,
כִּי לְעוֹלָם חַסְדּוֹ:

And Og, king of Bashan
—for His kindness is everlasting;

וְנָתַן אַרְצָם לְנַחֲלָה,
כִּי לְעוֹלָם חַסְדּוֹ:

And gave their land as an inheritance
—for His kindness is everlasting;

נַחֲלָה לְיִשְׂרָאֵל עַבְדּוֹ,
כִּי לְעוֹלָם חַסְדּוֹ:

An inheritance to Israel, His servant
—for His kindness is everlasting;

שֶׁבְּשִׁפְלֵנוּ זָכַר לָנוּ,
כִּי לְעוֹלָם חַסְדּוֹ:

Who remembered us in our lowliness
—for His kindness is everlasting;

וַיִּפְרְקֵנוּ מִצָּרֵינוּ,
כִּי לְעוֹלָם חַסְדּוֹ:

And delivered us from our oppressors
—for His kindness is everlasting;

נֹתֵן לֶחֶם לְכָל־בָּשָׂר,
כִּי לְעוֹלָם חַסְדּוֹ:

Who gives food to all flesh
—for His kindness is everlasting;

הוֹדוּ לְאֵל הַשָּׁמַיִם,
כִּי לְעוֹלָם חַסְדּוֹ:

Give thanks to the God of the heavens
—for His kindness is everlasting.

הַלֵּל

נִשְׁמַת כָּל־חַי | The Soul

תְּבָרֵךְ אֶת־שִׁמְךָ יְהֹוָה אֱלֹהֵינוּ, וְרוּחַ כָּל־בָּשָׂר תְּפָאֵר וּתְרוֹמֵם זִכְרְךָ מַלְכֵּנוּ תָּמִיד. מִן־הָעוֹלָם וְעַד־הָעוֹלָם אַתָּה אֵל, וּמִבַּלְעָדֶיךָ אֵין לָנוּ מֶלֶךְ גּוֹאֵל וּמוֹשִׁיעַ פּוֹדֶה וּמַצִּיל וּמְפַרְנֵס וּמְרַחֵם בְּכָל־עֵת צָרָה וְצוּקָה, אֵין לָנוּ מֶלֶךְ אֶלָּא אַתָּה: אֱלֹהֵי הָרִאשׁוֹנִים וְהָאַחֲרוֹנִים, אֱלוֹהַּ כָּל־בְּרִיּוֹת, אֲדוֹן כָּל־תּוֹלָדוֹת, הַמְהֻלָּל בְּרֹב הַתִּשְׁבָּחוֹת, הַמְנַהֵג

of every living thing shall bless Your Name, God, our God. And the spirit of all flesh will glorify and exalt Your remembrance at all times, our King. From eternity to eternity You are God, and besides You we have no king, redeemer, savior, deliverer, liberator, sustainer, and source of mercy in every time of trouble and distress. We have no King but You. God of the first and of the last, God of all creatures, Master of all events, Who is extolled with many praises; Who guides His

A Gift for a King

This prayer first expresses our inability to adequately praise God: "Even if our mouths were filled with song like the sea...we still could not sufficiently thank You." Yet, a few lines later, we say, "Therefore, the limbs that You have set within us...will thank, bless, praise, adore, exalt...."

How do we explain this seeming contradiction? Are we able to praise God or are we not?

An answer is given by way of a parable. There was once a king who was lost in the forest and couldn't find his way back to the palace. A simple man discovered the king and showed him the way. The king was very grateful, and he sent the man a gift—a set of earthenware dishes, which although not particularly valuable was much nicer than anything the poor man owned.

HALLEL

world with kindness and His creatures with compassion. God neither slumbers nor sleeps. He arouses the sleepers and wakens the slumberers, gives speech to the dumb, releases the bound, supports the fallen and straightens the bent. To You alone we give thanks. Even if our mouths were filled with song like the sea, and our tongues with melody like the multitudes of its waves, and our lips with praise like the breadth of the sky, and our eyes shining like the sun and the moon, and our hands spread out like the eagles of the skies, and our feet as swift as deer—we still could not sufficiently thank You God, our God, and God of our

עוֹלָמוֹ בְּחֶסֶד וּבְרִיּוֹתָיו בְּרַחֲמִים. וַיהוָה לֹא־יָנוּם וְלֹא יִישָׁן, הַמְעוֹרֵר יְשֵׁנִים וְהַמֵּקִיץ נִרְדָּמִים וְהַמֵּשִׂיחַ אִלְּמִים וְהַמַּתִּיר אֲסוּרִים וְהַסּוֹמֵךְ נוֹפְלִים וְהַזּוֹקֵף כְּפוּפִים, לְךָ לְבַדְּךָ אֲנַחְנוּ מוֹדִים. אִלּוּ פִינוּ מָלֵא שִׁירָה כַּיָּם וּלְשׁוֹנֵנוּ רִנָּה כַּהֲמוֹן גַּלָּיו, וְשִׂפְתוֹתֵינוּ שֶׁבַח כְּמֶרְחֲבֵי רָקִיעַ וְעֵינֵינוּ מְאִירוֹת כַּשֶּׁמֶשׁ וְכַיָּרֵחַ, וְיָדֵינוּ פְרוּשׂוֹת כְּנִשְׁרֵי שָׁמָיִם וְרַגְלֵינוּ קַלּוֹת כָּאַיָּלוֹת: אֵין אֲנַחְנוּ מַסְפִּיקִים לְהוֹדוֹת לְךָ יְהוָה אֱלֹהֵינוּ וֵאלֹהֵי אֲבוֹתֵינוּ וּלְבָרֵךְ אֶת־שְׁמֶךָ,

Sometime later, the king made an official trip through the forest again and decided to stop at the home of the man who had once saved him. When the man heard that the king would be visiting him, he scrambled to find a gift worthy of the king. But he was a poor man, and he didn't have anything befitting royalty, until he was finally struck by the idea of giving the very dishes the king had once given him.

When the man presented the dishes to the king, he explained, "These simple dishes are not befitting the king's greatness, but these are the dishes that Your Majesty gave me, and therefore this is the best that I can give, and I give it back to Your Majesty."

Similarly, we tell God that our abilities are limited, and we are therefore not able to adequately praise Him. All we can do is use what He gave us. Therefore, whatever it is that we do have, we give back to God in praise.

עַל־אַחַת מֵאֶלֶף אֶלֶף אַלְפֵי אֲלָפִים וְרִבֵּי רְבָבוֹת פְּעָמִים הַטּוֹבוֹת שֶׁעָשִׂיתָ עִם אֲבוֹתֵינוּ וְעִמָּנוּ: מִמִּצְרַיִם גְּאַלְתָּנוּ יְהֹוָה אֱלֹהֵינוּ, וּמִבֵּית עֲבָדִים פְּדִיתָנוּ. בְּרָעָב זַנְתָּנוּ וּבְשָׂבָע כִּלְכַּלְתָּנוּ, מֵחֶרֶב הִצַּלְתָּנוּ וּמִדֶּבֶר מִלַּטְתָּנוּ, וּמֵחֳלָיִם רָעִים וְנֶאֱמָנִים דִּלִּיתָנוּ: עַד־הֵנָּה עֲזָרוּנוּ רַחֲמֶיךָ וְלֹא־עֲזָבוּנוּ חֲסָדֶיךָ, וְאַל־תִּטְּשֵׁנוּ יְהֹוָה אֱלֹהֵינוּ לָנֶצַח: עַל־כֵּן אֵבָרִים שֶׁפִּלַּגְתָּ בָּנוּ וְרוּחַ וּנְשָׁמָה שֶׁנָּפַחְתָּ בְּאַפֵּינוּ וְלָשׁוֹן אֲשֶׁר שַׂמְתָּ בְּפִינוּ: הֵן הֵם יוֹדוּ וִיבָרְכוּ וִישַׁבְּחוּ וִיפָאֲרוּ וִירוֹמְמוּ וְיַעֲרִיצוּ וְיַקְדִּישׁוּ וְיַמְלִיכוּ אֶת־שִׁמְךָ מַלְכֵּנוּ: כִּי כָל־פֶּה לְךָ יוֹדֶה וְכָל־לָשׁוֹן לְךָ תִשָּׁבַע, וְכָל־בֶּרֶךְ

forebears, or bless Your name properly for even one of the thousand thousands of millions, and many myriads of favors that You have done for our ancestors and us. You have redeemed us from Egypt, God, our God, and You have freed us from the house of bondage. You have fed us during famine and nourished us in plenty. You have saved us from the sword, rescued us from pestilence, and raised us from foul and lingering diseases. Until now Your mercies have helped us, and Your kindnesses have not forsaken us; and, God our God, You will never abandon us. Therefore, the limbs that You have set within us, the spirit and soul that You breathed into our nostrils, and the tongue that You have placed in our mouth—they shall all thank, bless, praise, adore, exalt, glorify, sanctify, and proclaim the sovereignty of

Surrender and Acceptance

"Every knee will bend to You." Bending the knee and bowing are two different expressions of submission.[81] The difference between them is that when one bends their knee, their head is still held straight up. When one bows, they put their head down to the same level as their feet.

There are two levels of surrender before God. The first is simply an admission that God is more powerful than us, and,

HALLEL

Your Name, our King. For to You every mouth will offer thanks, every tongue will swear by You, every knee will bend to You, all who stand upright will bow down before You, all hearts will fear You, and every innermost part will sing praise to Your name, as the verse states: "All my bones will say, 'God, who is like You, Who saves the poor from one stronger than him, the poor and the needy from one who would rob him!'" Who can be likened to You, who can be equaled to You, who can be compared to You? The great, mighty, awesome God; the Supreme God, owner of heaven and earth. We will acclaim You, praise You, and glorify You, and we will bless Your holy name, as the verse states: "A Psalm by David. Bless God, my soul, and all that is within me His holy name."

לְךָ תִכְרַע וְכָל־קוֹמָה לְפָנֶיךָ תִשְׁתַּחֲוֶה. וְכָל לְבָבוֹת יִירָאוּךָ וְכָל־קֶרֶב וּכְלָיוֹת יְזַמְּרוּ לִשְׁמֶךָ, כַּדָּבָר שֶׁכָּתוּב: כָּל עַצְמוֹתַי תֹּאמַרְנָה, יְהֹוָה מִי כָמוֹךָ, מַצִּיל עָנִי מֵחָזָק מִמֶּנּוּ וְעָנִי וְאֶבְיוֹן מִגֹּזְלוֹ: מִי יִדְמֶה־לָּךְ וּמִי יִשְׁוֶה־לָּךְ וּמִי יַעֲרָךְ־לָךְ, הָאֵל הַגָּדוֹל הַגִּבּוֹר וְהַנּוֹרָא אֵל עֶלְיוֹן קֹנֵה שָׁמַיִם וָאָרֶץ: נְהַלֶּלְךָ וּנְשַׁבֵּחֲךָ וּנְפָאֶרְךָ וּנְבָרֵךְ אֶת־שֵׁם קָדְשֶׁךָ. כָּאָמוּר: לְדָוִד, בָּרְכִי נַפְשִׁי אֶת־יְהֹוָה, וְכָל־קְרָבַי אֶת־שֵׁם קָדְשׁוֹ:

therefore, although we may have a different understanding of what is good for us, we will defer to His wisdom. A deeper level of submission is where we lower our heads to the level of our feet and admit that we know nothing.

True surrender before God means not only do I accept that God's plan for me is better than my own, but that I know nothing at all of what is truly good for me. However, my loving and omnipotent Father in heaven surely does.

הָאֵל בְּתַעֲצֻמוֹת עֻזֶּךָ. הַגָּדוֹל בִּכְבוֹד שְׁמֶךָ. הַגִּבּוֹר לָנֶצַח וְהַנּוֹרָא בְּנוֹרְאוֹתֶיךָ. הַמֶּלֶךְ הַיּוֹשֵׁב עַל כִּסֵּא רָם וְנִשָּׂא:

שׁוֹכֵן עַד מָרוֹם וְקָדוֹשׁ שְׁמוֹ. וְכָתוּב: רַנְּנוּ צַדִּיקִים בַּיהֹוָה, לַיְשָׁרִים נָאוָה תְהִלָּה: בְּפִי יְשָׁרִים תִּתְהַלָּל. וּבְדִבְרֵי צַדִּיקִים תִּתְבָּרַךְ. וּבִלְשׁוֹן חֲסִידִים תִּתְרוֹמָם. וּבְקֶרֶב קְדוֹשִׁים תִּתְקַדָּשׁ:

וּבְמַקְהֲלוֹת רִבְבוֹת עַמְּךָ בֵּית יִשְׂרָאֵל בְּרִנָּה יִתְפָּאֵר שִׁמְךָ מַלְכֵּנוּ בְּכָל־דּוֹר וָדוֹר. שֶׁכֵּן חוֹבַת כָּל־הַיְצוּרִים, לְפָנֶיךָ יְהֹוָה אֱלֹהֵינוּ וֵאלֹהֵי אֲבוֹתֵינוּ לְהוֹדוֹת לְהַלֵּל לְשַׁבֵּחַ לְפָאֵר לְרוֹמֵם לְהַדֵּר לְבָרֵךְ לְעַלֵּה וּלְקַלֵּס, עַל כָּל־דִּבְרֵי שִׁירוֹת וְתִשְׁבְּחוֹת דָּוִד בֶּן־יִשַׁי עַבְדְּךָ מְשִׁיחֶךָ:

יִשְׁתַּבַּח שִׁמְךָ
לָעַד מַלְכֵּנוּ הָאֵל הַמֶּלֶךְ הַגָּדוֹל וְהַקָּדוֹשׁ בַּשָּׁמַיִם וּבָאָרֶץ. כִּי לְךָ נָאֶה יְהֹוָה אֱלֹהֵינוּ וֵאלֹהֵי אֲבוֹתֵינוּ: שִׁיר וּשְׁבָחָה הַלֵּל וְזִמְרָה עֹז וּמֶמְשָׁלָה נֶצַח גְּדֻלָּה

You are God in the power of Your strength; great in the honor of Your name, mighty forever, and awesome in terror of Your deeds; the King Who sits upon a lofty and exalted throne.

Dwelling for eternity, high and holy is His name, as the verse states: "You righteous, rejoice in God; it befits the upright to offer praise." By the mouth of the upright You are praised, by the words of the righteous You are blessed, by the tongue of the pious You are exalted, and among the holy ones You are sanctified.

In the assemblies of the multitudes of Your people, the House of Israel, shall Your Name, our King, be glorified with song in every generation. For such is the obligation of all creatures before You, God, our God and God of our ancestors: to thank, to laud, to praise, to glorify, to exalt, to adore, to bless, to extol, and to honor You, beyond all the words of songs and praises of David son of Jesse, Your anointed servant.

May Your Name
be praised forever, our King, the great and holy God and King, in heaven and on earth. For You, God, our God and God of our ancestors, befit song and praise, accolade and hymn, strength and dominion, victory, fame, and

HALLEL

might, glory, splendor, holiness and sovereignty; blessings and thanksgivings from now to eternity. Blessed are You, God, Almighty King, great in praises, God of thanksgivings, Master of wonders, Who chooses songs of praise; King, God, life of all worlds.

וּגְבוּרָה תְּהִלָּה וְתִפְאֶרֶת קְדֻשָּׁה וּמַלְכוּת. בְּרָכוֹת וְהוֹדָאוֹת מֵעַתָּה וְעַד עוֹלָם: בָּרוּךְ אַתָּה יְהֹוָה, אֵל מֶלֶךְ גָּדוֹל בַּתִּשְׁבָּחוֹת, אֵל הַהוֹדָאוֹת, אֲדוֹן הַנִּפְלָאוֹת, הַבּוֹחֵר בְּשִׁירֵי זִמְרָה, מֶלֶךְ אֵל חֵי הָעוֹלָמִים:

Hold the cup in your right hand.

Blessed are You, God, our God, King of the universe, Who creates the fruit of the vine.

בָּרוּךְ אַתָּה יְהֹוָה אֱלֹהֵינוּ מֶלֶךְ הָעוֹלָם, בּוֹרֵא פְּרִי הַגָּפֶן:

- Recline to the left and drink the cup (as before)
- After drinking the fourth cup, recite the following blessing:

Blessed are You, God our God, King of the universe, for the vine and the fruit of the vine, for the produce of the field, and for the precious, good, and ample land that You have favored and given as an inheritance to our ancestors, to eat of its fruit and be sated by its goodness. Have mercy please, God, our God, on Israel, Your people; on Jerusalem, Your city; on Zion, the abode of Your glory; on Your altar; and on

בָּרוּךְ אַתָּה יְהֹוָה אֱלֹהֵינוּ מֶלֶךְ הָעוֹלָם, עַל־הַגֶּפֶן וְעַל־פְּרִי הַגֶּפֶן וְעַל־תְּנוּבַת הַשָּׂדֶה וְעַל־אֶרֶץ חֶמְדָּה טוֹבָה וּרְחָבָה שֶׁרָצִיתָ וְהִנְחַלְתָּ לַאֲבוֹתֵינוּ לֶאֱכוֹל מִפִּרְיָהּ וְלִשְׂבֹּעַ מִטּוּבָהּ. רַחֶם־נָא יְהֹוָה אֱלֹהֵינוּ עַל־יִשְׂרָאֵל עַמֶּךָ וְעַל־יְרוּשָׁלַיִם עִירֶךָ וְעַל־צִיּוֹן מִשְׁכַּן כְּבוֹדֶךָ וְעַל־מִזְבְּחֶךָ וְעַל־הֵיכָלֶךָ,

וּבְנֵה יְרוּשָׁלַיִם עִיר הַקֹּדֶשׁ בִּמְהֵרָה בְיָמֵינוּ וְהַעֲלֵנוּ לְתוֹכָהּ, וְשַׂמְּחֵנוּ בְּבִנְיָנָהּ וְנֹאכַל מִפִּרְיָהּ וְנִשְׂבַּע מִטּוּבָהּ, וּנְבָרֶכְךָ עָלֶיהָ בִּקְדֻשָּׁה וּבְטָהֳרָה,

(on Shabbos add)

וּרְצֵה וְהַחֲלִיצֵנוּ בְּיוֹם הַשַּׁבָּת הַזֶּה

וְשַׂמְּחֵנוּ בְּיוֹם חַג הַמַּצּוֹת הַזֶּה. כִּי אַתָּה יְהֹוָה טוֹב וּמֵטִיב לַכֹּל וְנוֹדֶה לְּךָ עַל־הָאָרֶץ וְעַל־פְּרִי הַגָּפֶן: בָּרוּךְ אַתָּה יְהֹוָה עַל־הָאָרֶץ וְעַל־פְּרִי הַגָּפֶן:

Your Temple. Rebuild Jerusalem, the holy city, speedily in our days. Bring us up into it, and let us rejoice in its reconstruction. Let us eat of its fruits and be sated in its goodness. We will bless You over it in holiness and purity; (on Shabbos add: may it please You to strengthen us on this Shabbos day) **and bring us joy on this day of the Festival of Matzos. For You, God, are good and do good to all, and we thank You for the Land and for the fruit of the vine. Blessed are You, God, for the Land and for the fruit of the vine.**

SEDER STEP 15 NIRTZAH

NIRTZAH

נִרְצָה חֲסַל סִדּוּר פֶּסַח כְּהִלְכָתוֹ, כְּכָל־מִשְׁפָּטוֹ וְחֻקָּתוֹ, כַּאֲשֶׁר זָכִינוּ לְסַדֵּר אוֹתוֹ, כֵּן נִזְכֶּה לַעֲשׂוֹתוֹ: זָךְ שׁוֹכֵן מְעוֹנָה, קוֹמֵם קְהַל עֲדַת מִי מָנָה, בְּקָרוֹב נַהֵל נִטְעֵי כַנָּה, פְּדוּיִים לְצִיּוֹן בְּרִנָּה:

Our Seder Has Been Accepted On High.
Our Pesach service is now completed in correct form with all its regulations and precepts. Just as we have had the privilege to celebrate it tonight, so may we merit to celebrate it in the future. O Pure One, Who dwells in heaven, raise up the gathering of Your innumerable people! Soon, lead them, "the plants of Your vine," as free ones to Zion in song.

לְשָׁנָה הַבָּאָה בִּירוּשָׁלָיִם:
Next year in Jerusalem!

Ultimate Freedom

We have just concluded celebrating our freedom, but we are acutely aware that there are greater levels of freedom that still remain for ourselves and more importantly for God's entire creation.

"Next year in Jerusalem" is the expression of our desire for the redemption of the entire world with the coming of Mashiach. May it be immediately.

ENDNOTES

1. Chinuch, Mitzvah 21
2. Mechilta and Rashi, Exodus 13:3
3. Tiferet Sheb'malchut, p. 326
4. Rabbi Yaakov Ben Yosef Reischer, Chok Yaakov, Orach Chaim 473:28
5. Big Book, p. 164
6. Ohel Yaakov, p. 57
7. Kol Bo, 50
8. Rabbi Yosef Yitzchak Schneersohn, Sefer Hasichot 5697, p. 239
9. See Haggadah Shel Pesach Im Likutei Taamim
10. Rabbi David Abudraham
11. Zohar II:136b
12. Deuteronomy 16:3
13. Talmud, Brachot 27b
14. Gevurot Hashem, Chapter 61
15. Deuteronomy 6:20
16. Mishnah, Pesachim 119b
17. Haggadah Shel Pesach Im Likutei Taamim
18. Exodus 12:26
19. See Sefer Hasharashim, Ta'am; Sefer Erkei Hakinuyim, Ta'am
20. Exodus 13:8
21. Birkat Chaim, Vol. 2, p. 127
22. Exodus 13:14
23. Ibid. 13:8
24. Ibid.
25. Talmud, Pesachim, 116a
26. Joshua 24:2–4
27. Genesis 15:13–14
28. Deuteronomy 26:5
29. Genesis 47:4
30. Deuteronomy 10:22
31. Exodus 1:7
32. Ezekiel 16:6–7
33. Genesis 31:43
34. Deuteronomy 10:22
35. Deuteronomy 26:6
36. Exodus 1:10
37. Exodus 1:11
38. Ibid. 13
39. Talmud, Sotah 11b; See Maharsha, Bamidbar Rabbah 15:20
40. Deuteronomy 26:7
41. Exodus 2:23
42. Ibid. 24
43. Ibid. 25
44. Ibid. 1:22
45. Ibid. 3:9
46. Deuteronomy 26:8
47. Exodus 12:12
48. Ibid. 9:3
49. I Chronicles 21:16
50. Deuteronomy 4:34
51. Exodus 4:17
52. Joel 3:3
53. Shemot Rabbah 12:4
54. The Rebbe, Rabbi Menachem Mendel Schneerson, Reshimot 27
55. Talmud, Brachot 63b; Shabbat 33b
56. Tzvi Latzaddik, Peninim, p. 425
57. Exodus 8:15
58. Ibid. 4:31
59. Psalms 78:49
60. See Rabbi Nissim Ben Reuven Of Gerona, Drashot HaRan 8, first introduction
61. Rabbi Shneur Zalman of Liadi (Alter Rebbe), Likkutei Torah, Tzav 16d
62. Exodus 12:27

ENDNOTES

63. Exodus 12:39
64. Ibid. 1:14
65. Numbers 33:1
66. Likkutei Torah, 88c; 89b
67. Exodus 13:8
68. Deuteronomy 6:23
69. Numbers 9:11
70. Rabbi Chaim Vital, Pri Eitz Chaim, Shaar Chag Hamatzot, chapters 5 and 7
71. P. 96
72. Tishbi, Afikoman
73. Big Book, p. 164
74. Psalms 79:6
75. See Rashi, Leviticus 26:42; Targum Yonatan Exodus 6:18
76. Rabbi Zelikman Binga, Mishnah Berura 480:10
77. Psalms 69:25
78. Lamentations 3:66
79. Haggadah Shel Pesach im Likutei Taamim, op. cit.
80. See Talmud, Niddah 31a
81. Rabbi David Abudraham, on Nishmat

PROVIDING INDIVIDUALIZED TREATMENT PROGRAMS FOR PEOPLE SUFFERING FROM TRAUMA, MENTAL HEALTH, & ADDICTION.

Call us or check out our site to learn more.
(877) 373-7040 | theheightstreatment.com

REDISCOVER A PASSION FOR PURPOSEFUL LIVING AT TRANSCEND'S MENTAL HEALTH & ADDICTION SUPPORTIVE LIVING HOMES IN LOS ANGELES, HOUSTON & NEW YORK.

If you or a loved one is struggling with mental health & addiction, call us to learn how we can help.
(800) 648-3906 | TranscendRecoveryCommunity.com

DEDICATED TO THE MEMORY OF
JEFF MOISHE KRAUS

Jeffs Place is a living entity dedicated to those struggling with substance use abuse, those in recovery and their loved ones. Jeff's Place is here to support all those who struggle to find a spiritual path to healthier living. Jeff's Place nurtures the key ingredients for recovery, it is a resource and a literal life saving space.

Jeff's Place was founded to help minimize stigma in the Jewish community around addiction and recovery. It is our vision that Jeff's Place will inspire more open conversation and that other Jewish organizations and synagogues will take our lead. Together, we will share the message that there is hope, save lives and ensure that everyone who is hurting can find healing.

Jeff's Place is an open, welcoming and safe environment to all those seeking support and guidance no matter religious background.

https://www.jeffsplaceatlanta.org/

DEDICATED TO THE MANY SUFFERING ADDICTS AND
THEIR FAMILIES WHO, DESPITE REPEATED SETBACKS,
NEVER GIVE UP HOPE.

ELI NASH

KEEP UP THE GOOD WORK.

D.H.

DEDICATED TO OUR CHILDREN FOR
HEALTH AND HAPPINESS!

NECHEMIA & RAIZEL SCHUSTERMAN

IN LOVING MEMORY OF
ARDEN ZINN
WHO UNCONDITIONALLY SUPPORTED
RECOVERY IN SO MANY INDIVIDUALS.

לזכר נשמת משה בן מנחם מענדל ע"ה

IN HONOR OF
רבקה מינדל בת פערל צירל

AN אשת חיל WITH TRUE DEDICATION.
MAY HASHEM CONTINUE TO BENTCH
HER WITH BROCHOS עד בלי די.